THE LAST RESORT

Martin Parr

THE LAST RESORT
40 YEARS ON

Produced to coincide with *The Last Resort, 40 Years On*, exhibited at the Martin Parr Foundation in Bristol, 2026. This exhibition and accompanying publication celebrate the remarkable career of Martin Parr (1952-2025).

The Last Resort, 40 Years On also marks the 40th anniversary of *The Last Resort*, first published and exhibited as a solo show in 1986. The original photobook was self-published by Martin Parr under Promenade Press and designed by Peter Brawne. Dewi Lewis went on to publish subsequent editions of the photobook in 1998 and 2009. The work was initially shown at Open Eye Gallery, Liverpool, in a joint exhibition with Tom Wood in the winter of 1985, ahead of Martin's landmark solo exhibition of *The Last Resort* at Serpentine Gallery, London, in 1986.

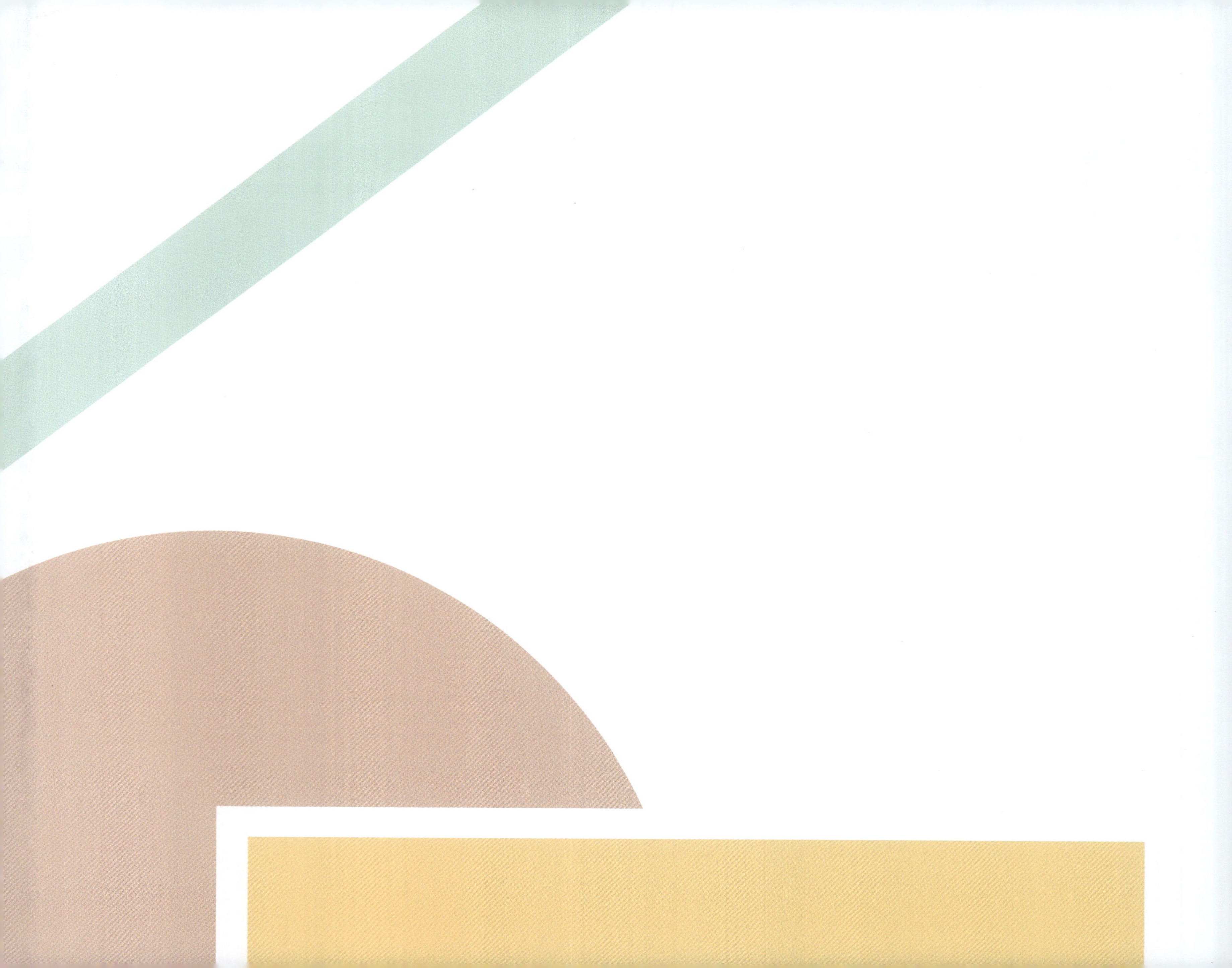

"The pictures from *The Last Resort* still hold very well. When I get to the Pearly Gates, those are the ones I'd probably get out first!"
Martin Parr

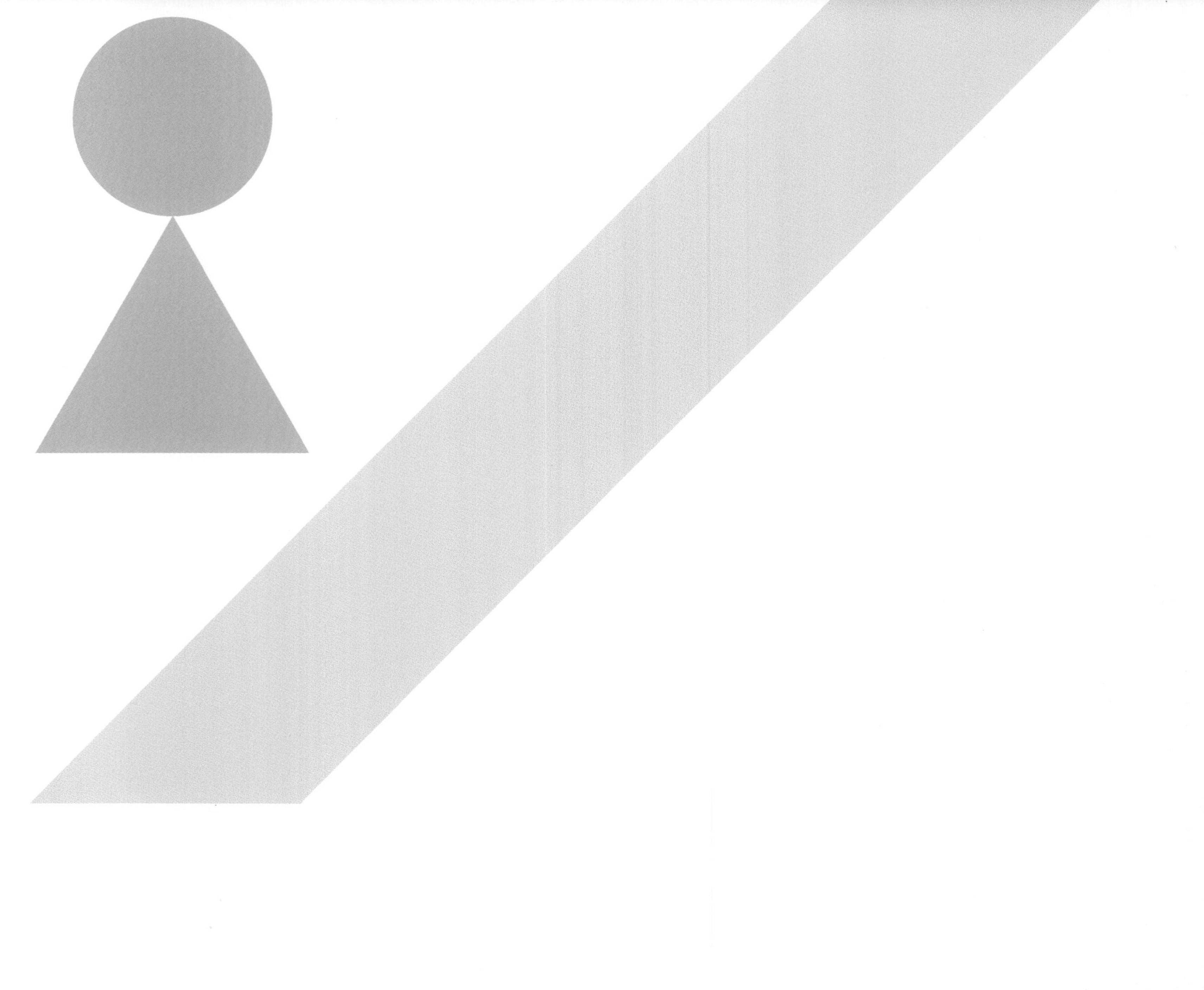

The Last Resort, 40 Years On
Isaac Blease

A number of factors aligned in the making of Martin Parr's *The Last Resort*. From moving to Wallasey with his wife Susie in 1982, a stone's throw from New Brighton where the hot summers of 1983 and 1984 brought huge crowds, to the arrival of the new Plaubel Makina W67 camera solidifying his move to colour—all in the charged political backdrop of the 1980s.

Revisiting the work now, forty years after its 1986 publication, it's easy to imagine it had a clear trajectory—though at the time, Martin was moving into uncharted territory. Arriving in Merseyside from Ireland, his work had received recognition through magazines such as Creative Camera and shows at Impressions and Half Moon Gallery. He'd also published his first book (*Bad Weather*, 1982), and was working on what would become his second (*A Fair Day: Photographs from the West of Ireland*, 1984). Yet a need to break with the conventions of his more wistful black and white imagery of the 1970s was building against a rising frustration with the humanist tradition in photography and its toothlessness against the vicious political and cultural reality of the 1980s.

New Brighton was an area bearing many tell-tale signs of Margaret Thatcher's Britain, etched into the fading grandeur of what was once a fashionable Victorian resort, originally built to rival Brighton in the South. When, in 1983, Martin began photographing what would become *The Last Resort*, Thatcher was entering her second term,

and the effects of cuts to industry and social services were being felt most acutely in the North. Liverpool had been declared effectively unfit for investment under the notorious "managed decline" policies, while regeneration projects such as Michael Heseltine's International Garden Festival, offered little more than cosmetic relief for areas and communities most vulnerable to economic change. In the original 1986 press release for *The Last Resort* book, minimal commentary is given to the photographs, instead a factual account of the area is reeled off, highlighting its mixed fortunes:

> '*Originally a watering-place for the wealthy merchants of Liverpool, New Brighton hit the peak of its popularity in the first two decades of this century. The tower, built in 1897, was actually higher than Blackpool's but had to be demolished after the first world war due to neglect. New Brighton's decline was accelerated in the 1960s when most of the sand disappeared because of tidal changes in the River Mersey. This was consolidated by the closure of the ferry service to Liverpool in 1971 and the demolition of the pier in 1978. Despite this, some notable features remain: the Lido outdoor swimming pool built in 1934, is one of the largest in Europe. There is also a fine promenade and The Palace amusement park.*' [1]

On this hallowed ground, heritage and culture collided with the stark economic downturn of the period, as the project subtly repositioned the seemingly untouchable institution of the British seaside resort as a frontier for the wider changes unfolding across the country. Through the architecture, amusements, and collective memories, holiday resorts occupied an outsized place in the national imagination. Once-booming Victorian destinations, their status had steadily diminished with the rise of affordable international travel, often becoming under-resourced and marginal places where fun and decadence sat in equal measure.

The reality Martin encountered in New Brighton clashed with the rose-tinted scenes depicted in the many postcards he had been collecting from significant resorts; *The Last Resort* book opens with the reproduction of a postcard from his collection of New Brighton. Central to the publicity machine around resorts and holidaymaking was John Hinde, who had built a postcard empire. His pioneering use of large-format colour transparencies, flash lighting, and intricate printing processes in the 1960s and 1970s is often cited as a key influence on Martin's move towards colour (fig. 1 & 2). The connection is further deepened by Hinde's work for Butlin's holiday camps, where Martin worked alongside friend and fellow photographer Daniel Meadows, as a 'Walkie' photographer during their holidays as students from Manchester Polytechnic (fig. 3).

With his move to colour, he began using 120 medium-format film and fill-in flash, working with the newly released Plaubel Makina W67—a lightweight camera combining Japanese and German engineering—and started by photographing urban areas of Liverpool and Merseyside (fig. 4). Meanwhile, he was still completing his last commission in black-and-white, for an Open Eye Gallery project entitled Connections. This series, which saw him focus on the Chinese

community in the area, was shown alongside John Davies, Vanley Burke, Jenny Wilson, John Hyatt, and Pete Clarke. The Chinatown series in 1984 marked the end of his work in monochrome (fig. 5).

What did remain from his black-and-white years (and forever on) was the influence of Tony Ray-Jones (fig. 6), whose compositional intelligence and acerbic eye for national customs and foibles helped shape Martin's early understandings of the medium. Yet when these spatially arranged, tragi-comic moments of human behaviour were combined with the detail of medium-format film, new layers of information began to assert themselves. Peripheral elements now demanded as much attention as the central motifs: a digestive biscuit balancing on the edge of a blue-chequered blanket, or a red plastic ice-cream stick beneath a shoe, each contributing to the main event.

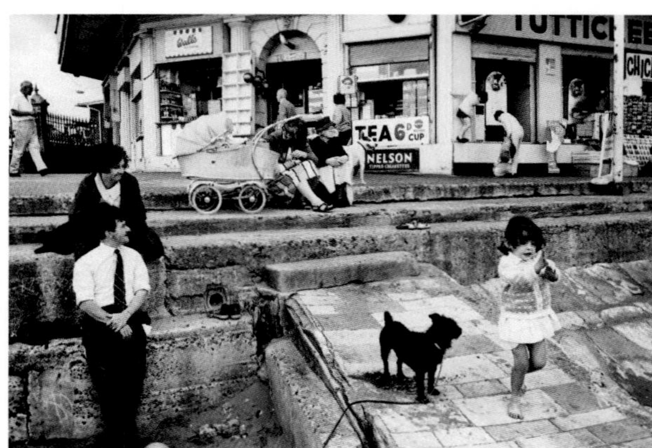

fig. 6 / Ramsgate, c.1968 © Board of Trustees of the Science Museum. Image by Tony Ray-Jones

Looking through Martin's contact sheets (which he printed himself in black and white due to the expense of colour printing at the time) reveals how he gravitated towards, and then stayed within, a

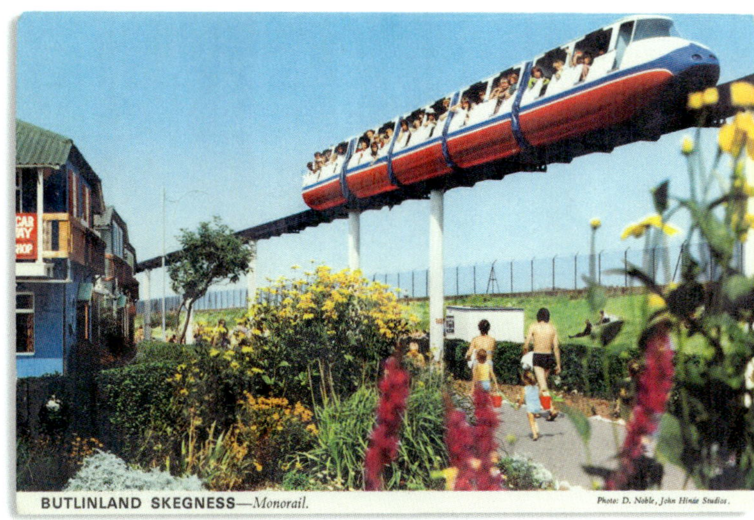

fig. 1. The Monorail at Butlin's Holiday Camp, Skegness - Photograph by David Noble for John Hinde Studios Ltd. reproduced on a postcard © The John Hinde Archive / Mary Evans

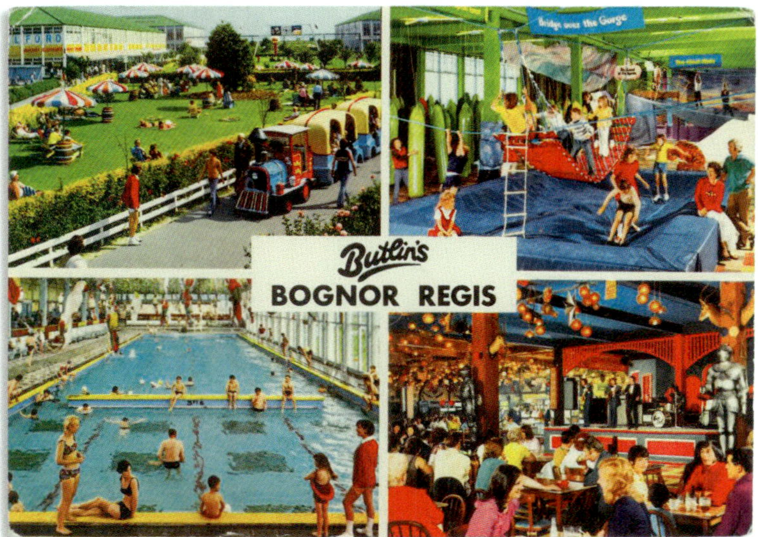

fig. 2. Four views of the Butlin's Holiday Camp at Bognor Regis - Photographs by John Hinde Studios Ltd. reproduced on a mulit-view postcard © The John Hinde Archive / Mary Evans

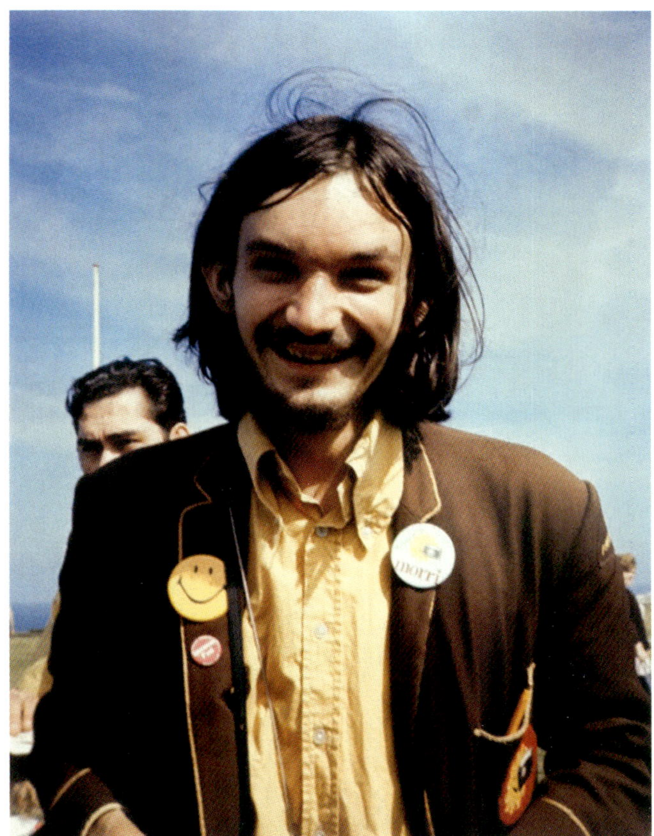

fig. 3. Martin Parr at Butlin's, Filey, England, 1972
© Martin Parr Collection / Magnum Photos

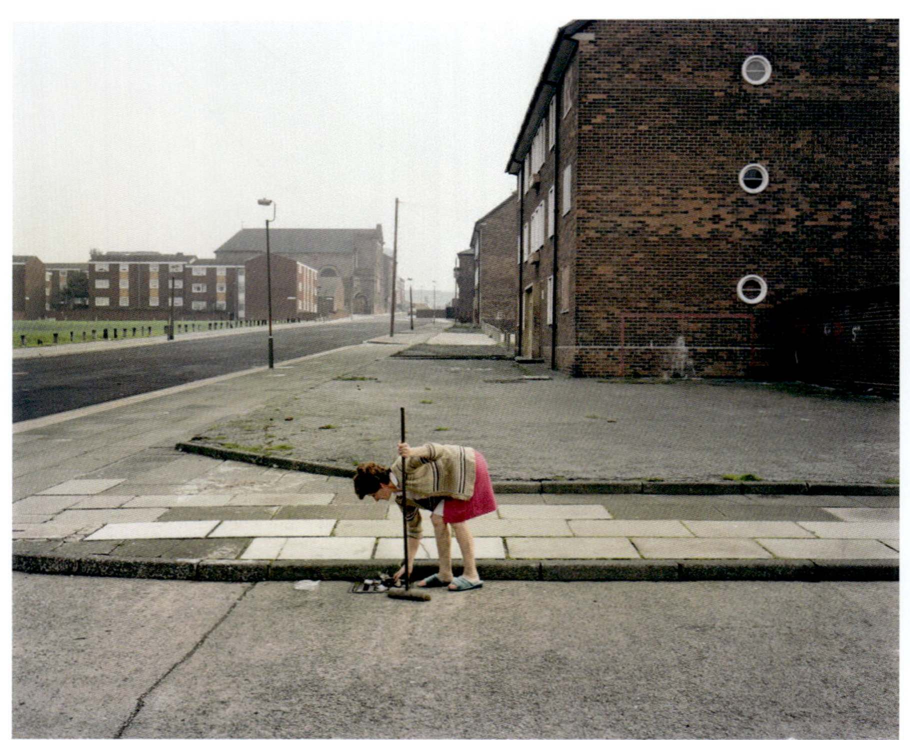

fig. 4. Liverpool, England, 1984 © Martin Parr / Magnum Photos

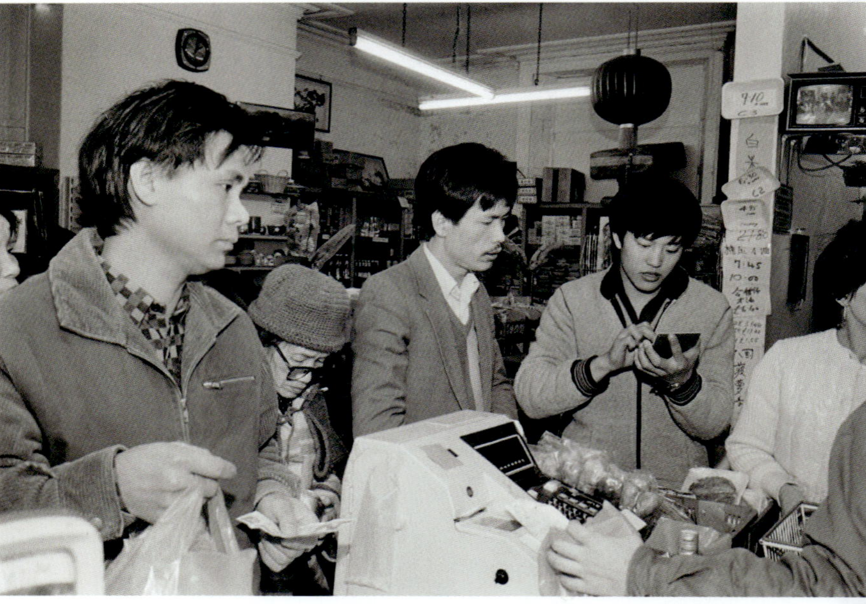

fig. 5. Cheung Wah Supermarket, Chinatown, Nelson Street, Liverpool, England, 1985
© Martin Parr / Magnum Photos

childhood adventure, new lovers and ageing couples. It was all preserved by a kiss of fill-in flash—a device effectively used by Chris Killip and Graham Smith in their earlier depictions of the North East of England. The use of flash provided an intriguing reference point for the artist's position in relation to subject, introducing a subtle detachment that added new narratives and tensions while dispelling the notion of an objective observer.

In the winter of 1985, Neil Burgess, who was then director at Open Eye Gallery, organised the first showing of Martin's New Brighton images, in a two-person exhibition with Tom Wood, who had been working in the area since the late 1970s. The exhibition titled *The Last Resort* was a success, complete with a Punch and Judy show and a special stick of rock made for the opening, with guests bringing lilos and wearing swimming costumes (fig. 8).

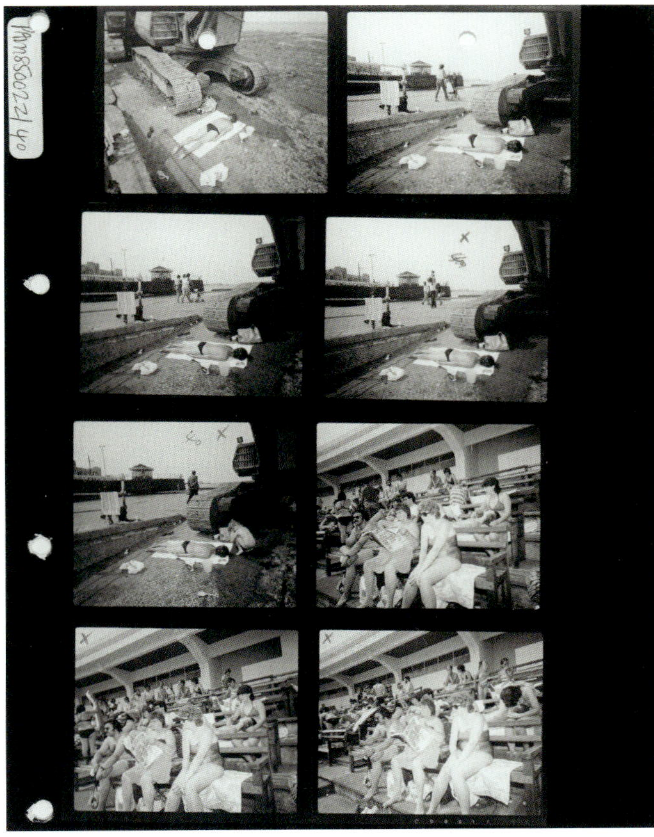

fig. 7. Martin Parr contact sheet from *The Last Resort*, 1983-85
© Martin Parr Collection / Magnum Photos

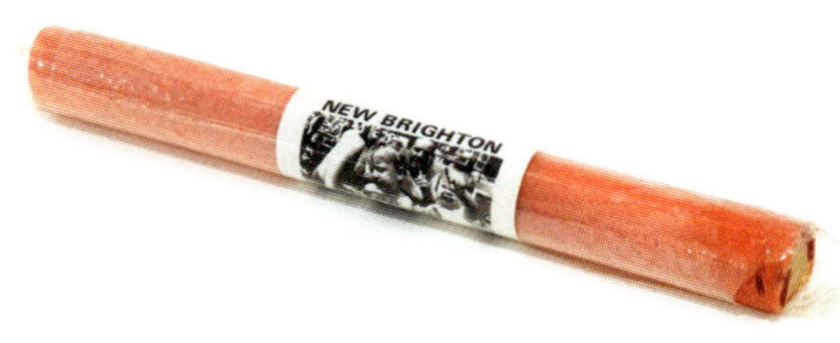

fig. 8. *The Last Resort* rock featuring an image by Tom Wood, made for the original Open Eye Gallery exhibition opening, 1985. © Martin Parr Collection / Magnum Photos

particular scene (fig. 7). Recognising a site of potential, he lined up compositions and waited for action, for people to enter this newly formed stage set, orchestrating a soap opera of the everyday. Through this, his images of New Brighton became densely packed with markers and suggestions—a dizzying array of information ranging from litter and building debris to teenage boredom,

Talks of a joint publication took place, but ultimately Martin went it alone, securing an Arts Council of Great Britain grant of £5,300 through Barry Lane[2], whose funding had supported many key independent publications by artists such as Jo Spence and Paul Graham. Martin self-published under his own imprint; Promenade Press, while distribution was covered by Phaidon. He enlisted designer Peter Brawne, who he'd previously worked with on *A Fair Day*, to produce the design, which was very much of its time, with bold colours, elaborate type, and showy flourishes—yet one that convincingly frames the images through the visual language of the seaside and its insignia.

The book launched in the summer of 1986, at the same time as the work was being exhibited at the Serpentine Gallery (fig. 9). Despite its relatively short run (23 Jul – 3 Aug), the exhibition received a considerable response, provoking a mixture of reviews. In many cases critics accused Parr of cruelty and condescension, particularly towards the working class. As is so often the case with photography, the artist became a proxy for the viewer's own prejudices, a moment which was radically intensified by the fraught class politics and relationships of the mid-1980s. The work was unflinching, and at times revealing in uncomfortable ways; but in its clear-sighted honesty a portrait of the time was shown, from the comical and endearing to the sad and terrifying. As the book's blurb states, 'few of the questions posed are easily answerable'[3], a point many missed at the time.

Like much of his work, Martin was effectively photographing what was on his doorstep, and that which he would often describe as 'ordinary'. He spoke about being more concerned with images of everyday events that happen to all of us; waiting in a queue, carrying shopping home from the supermarket, a crying baby, as opposed to focusing on the extreme events in society—although knowingly, the political was always looming in the background. This was to become one of Martin's motifs, through which he consistently found details that revealed moments of truth within the changing habits and trajectories of society.

'There's no such thing as the perfect picture, every day you go out, you hope to get one of them, and most of the time you don't. But you have to have that belief early in the morning before you go out that this could be the day when something happens.' [4]

As an artist he never wavered in his quest for that elusive image; the one where everything comes together. *The Last Resort* contains a number of those 'one-offs', yet perhaps the greatest outlier was always Martin himself. He leaves behind a rich and varied photographic legacy, one that will continue to reveal our strange and unpredictable ways for many years to come.

List of references:
1. Press release for *The Last Resort* by Martin Parr. Promenade Press, 1986.
2. Creative Camera, 2/1987, p. 39.
3. *The Last Resort.* Martin Parr, Promenade Press, 1986.
4. *I Am Martin Parr.* Directed by Lee Shulman, Dogwoof, 2024. Martin Parr speaking on a visit to New Brighton in 2024, 16:22–16:36.

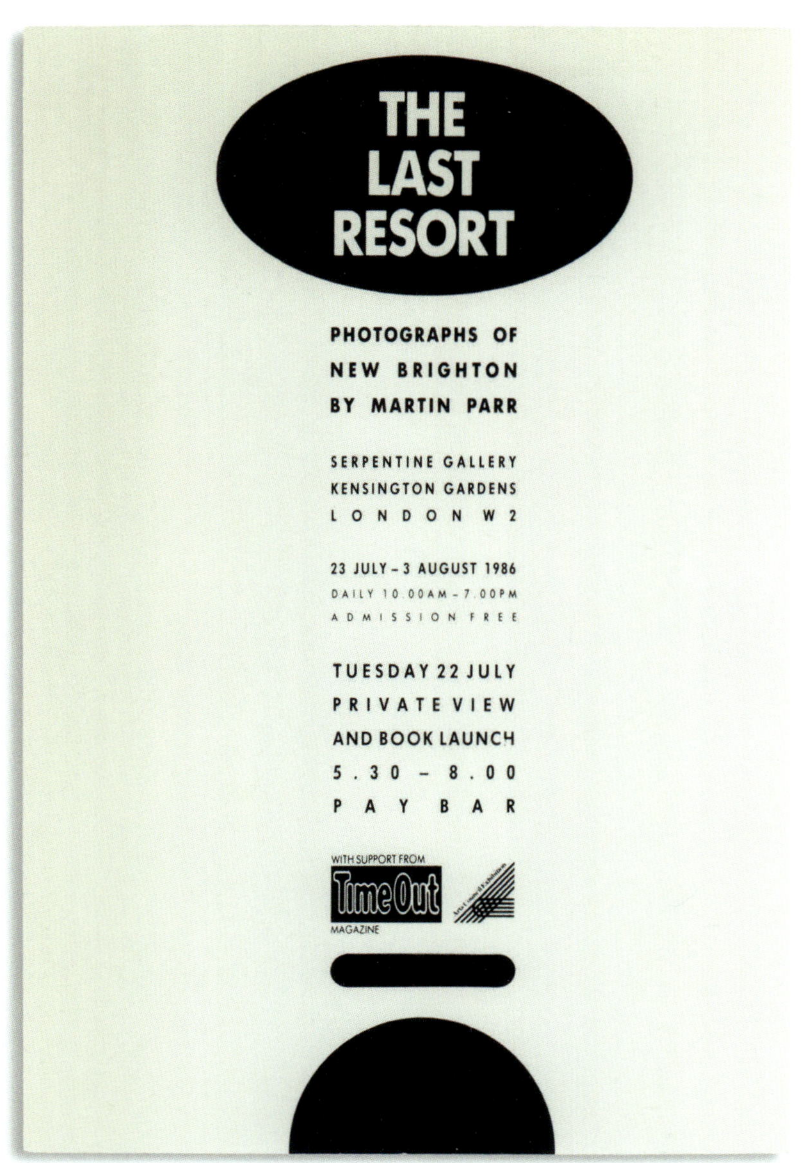

fig. 9. *The Last Resort* opening invitation for the Serpentine Gallery exhibition, designed by Peter Brawne, 1986 © Martin Parr Collection / Magnum Photos

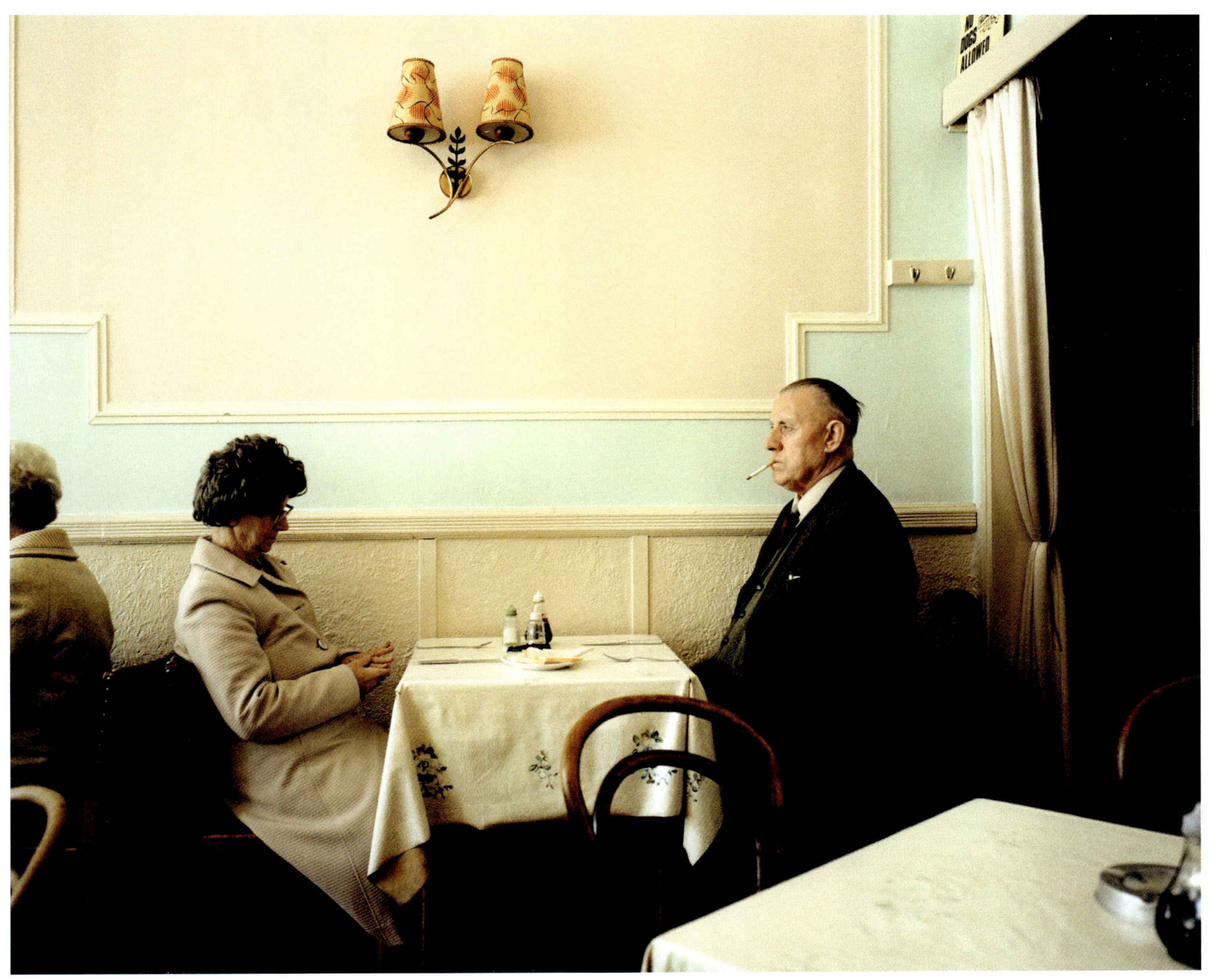

NO
DOGS
ALLOWED

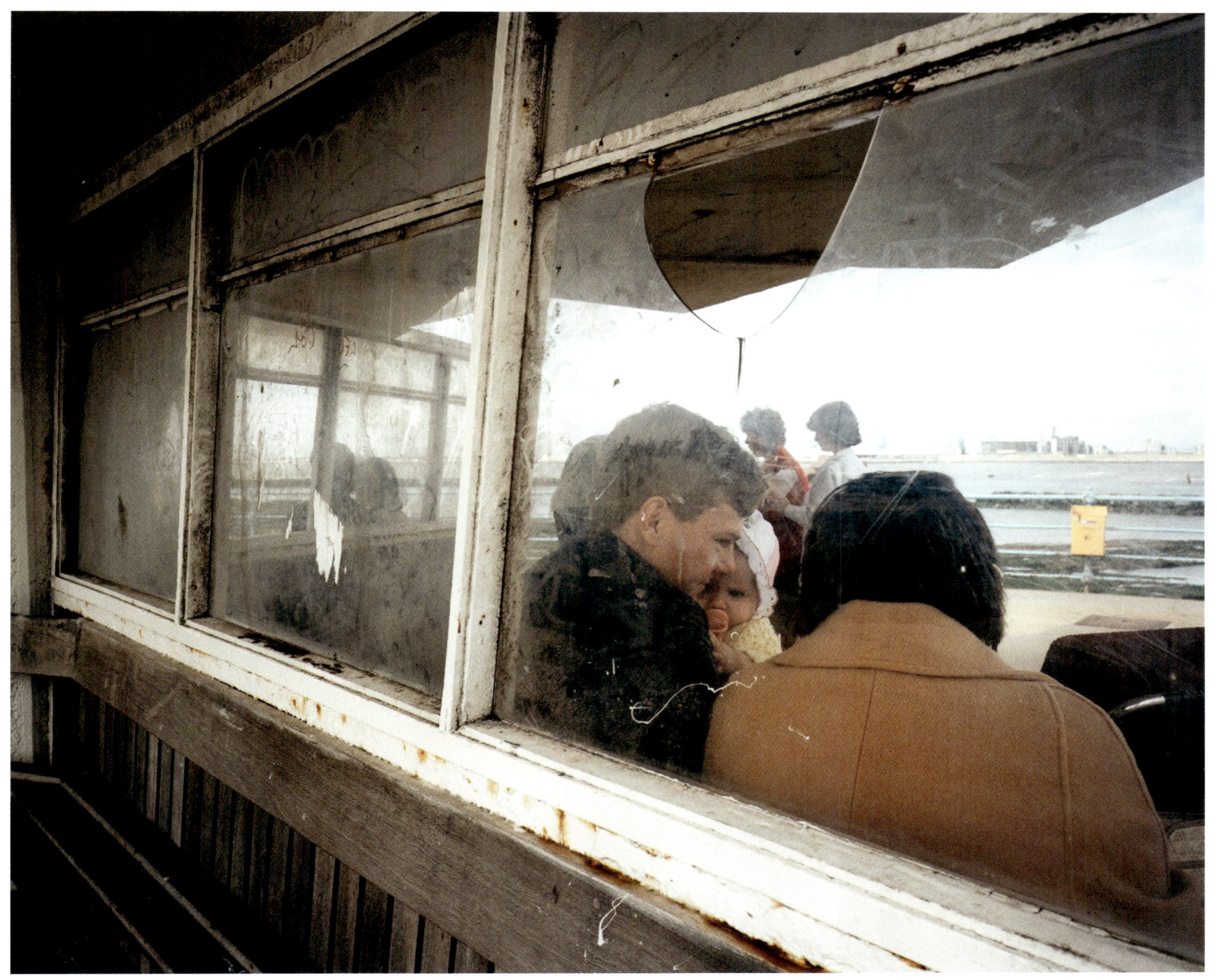

17

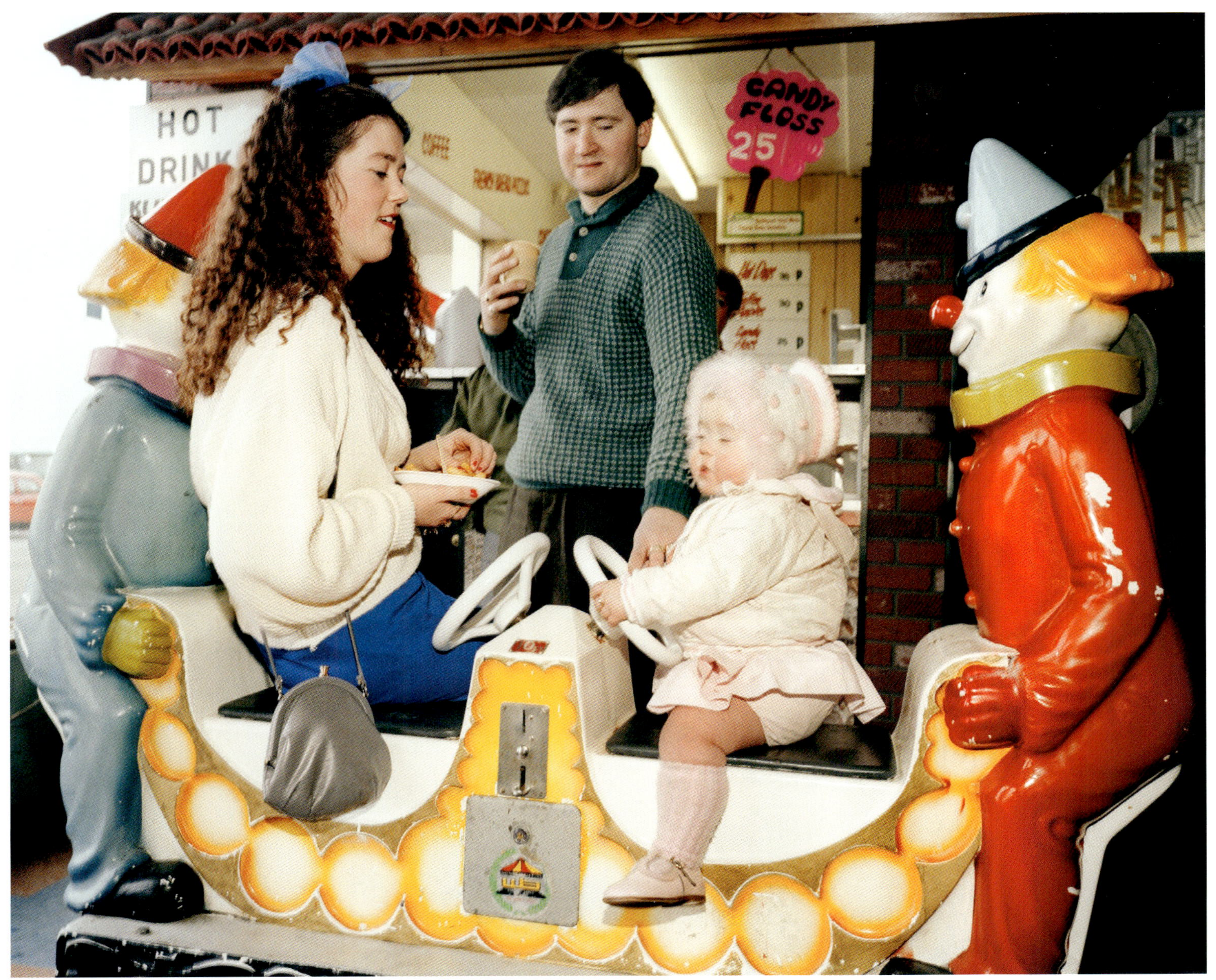
HOT
DRINK
COFFEE
CANDY
FLOSS
25

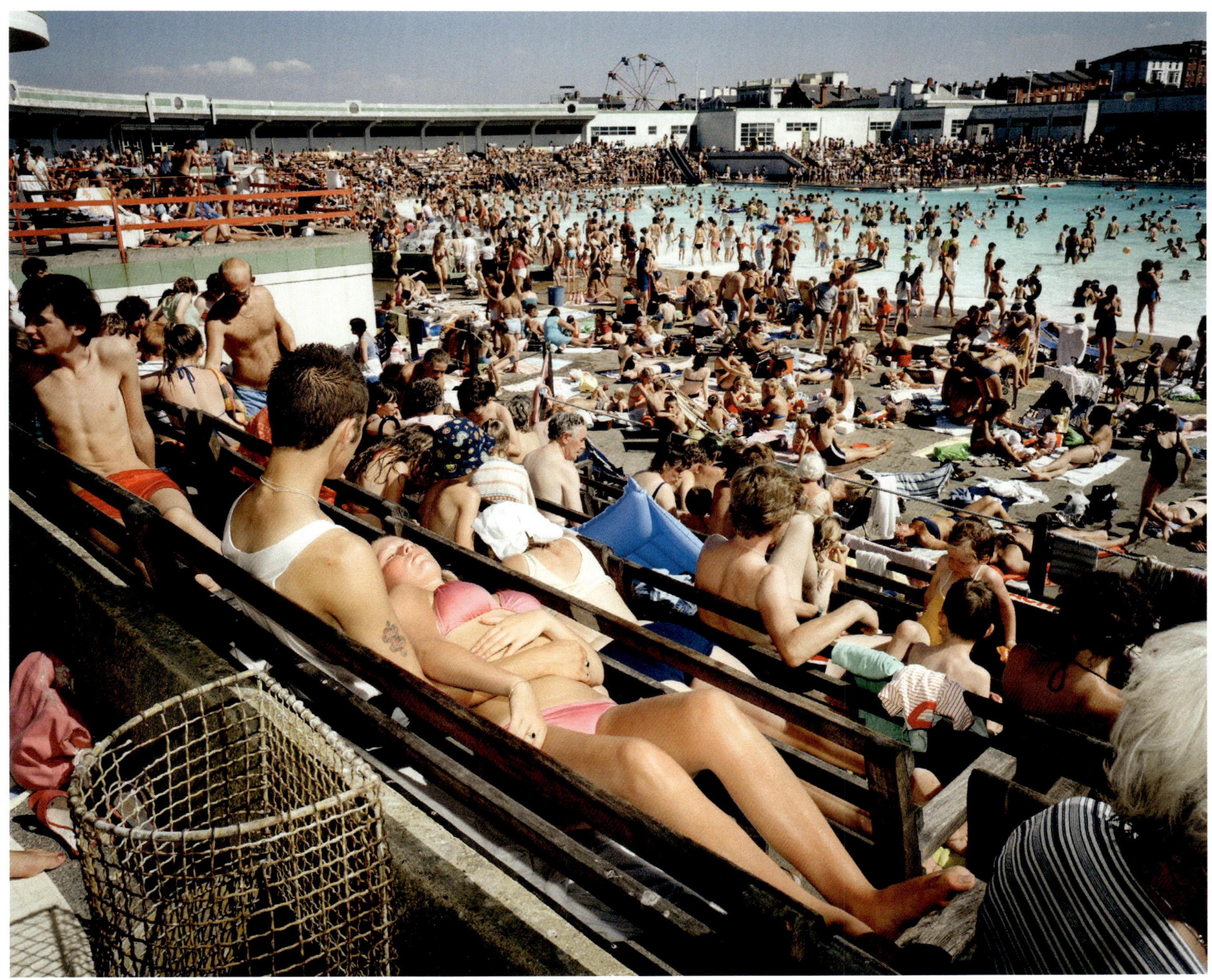

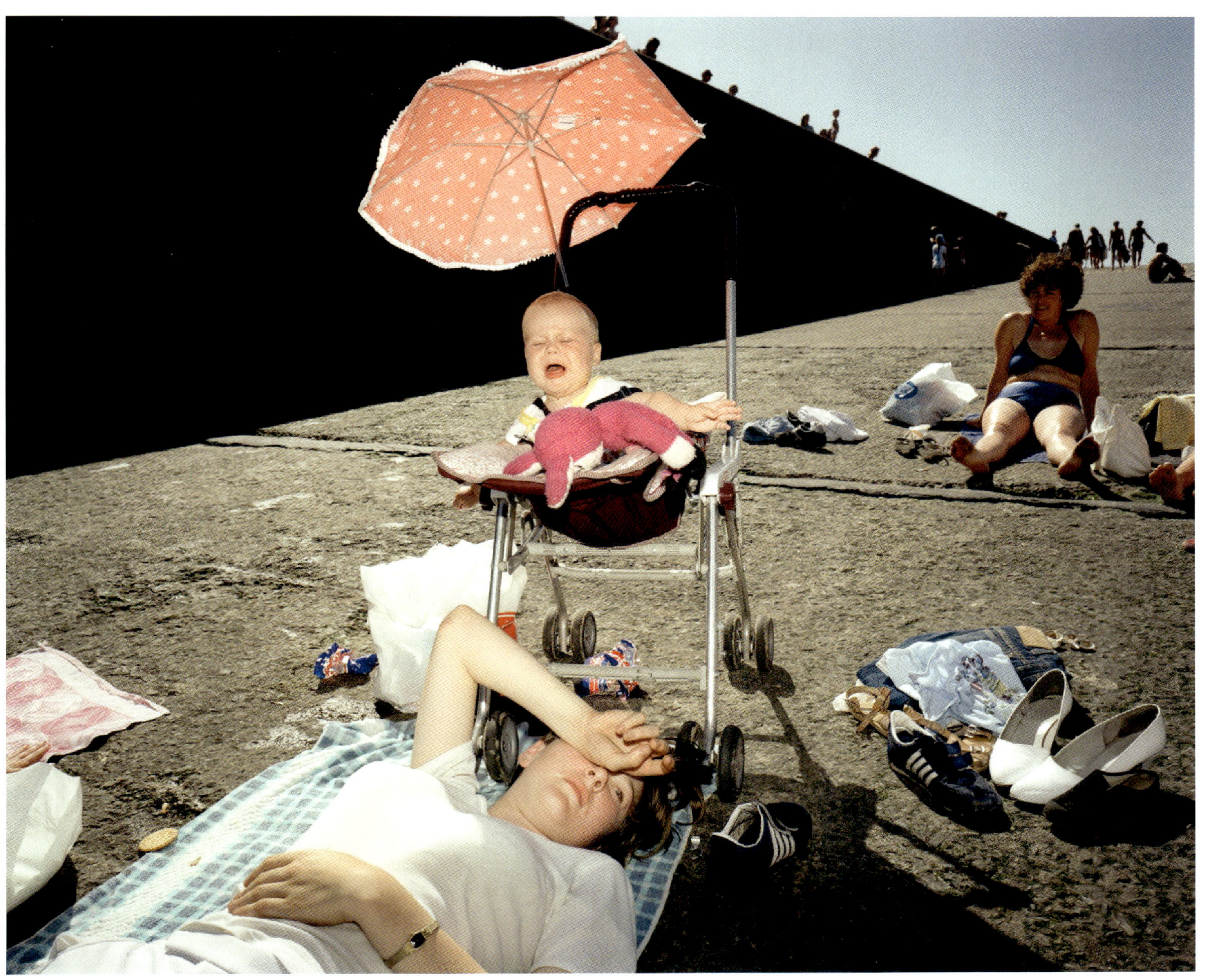

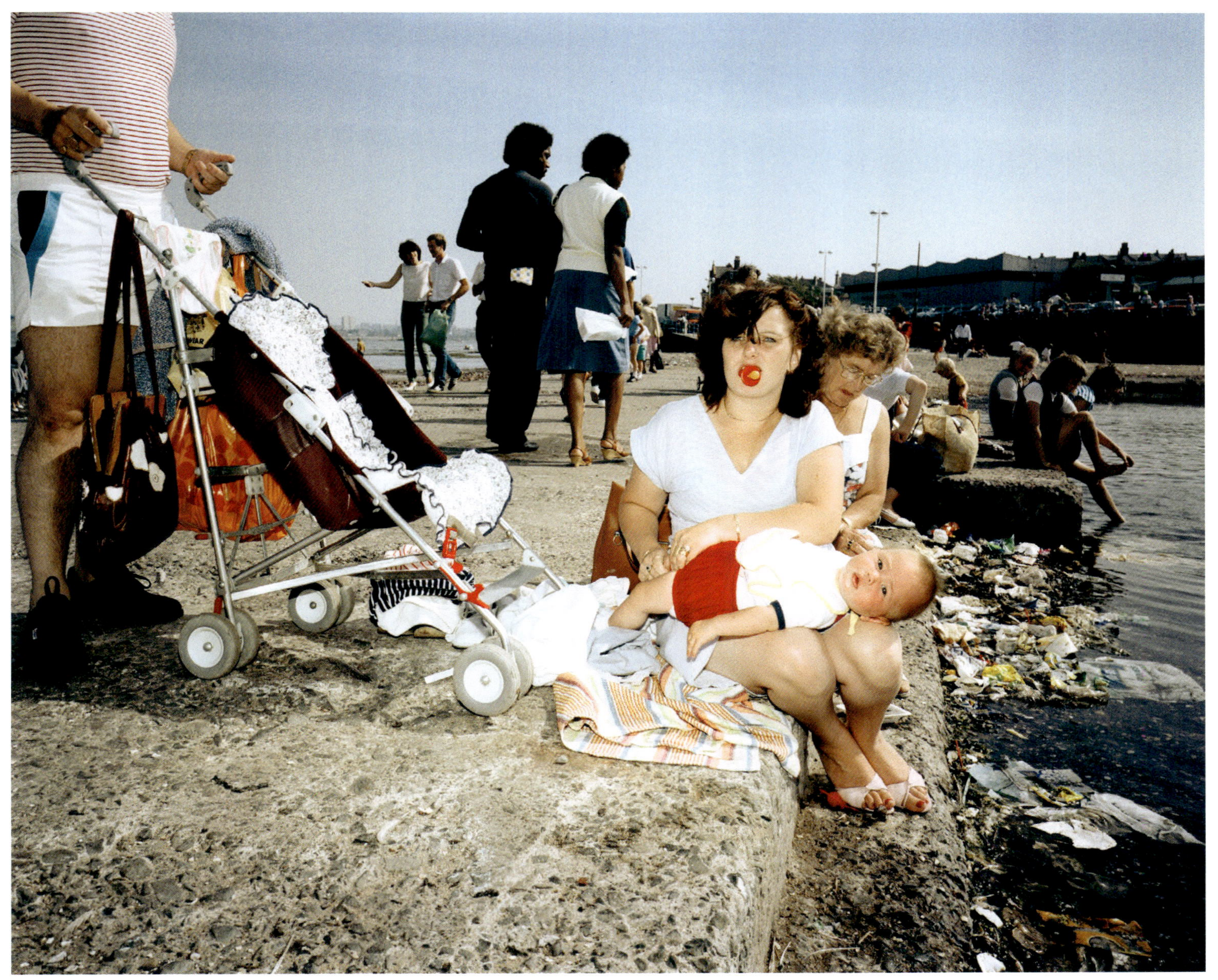

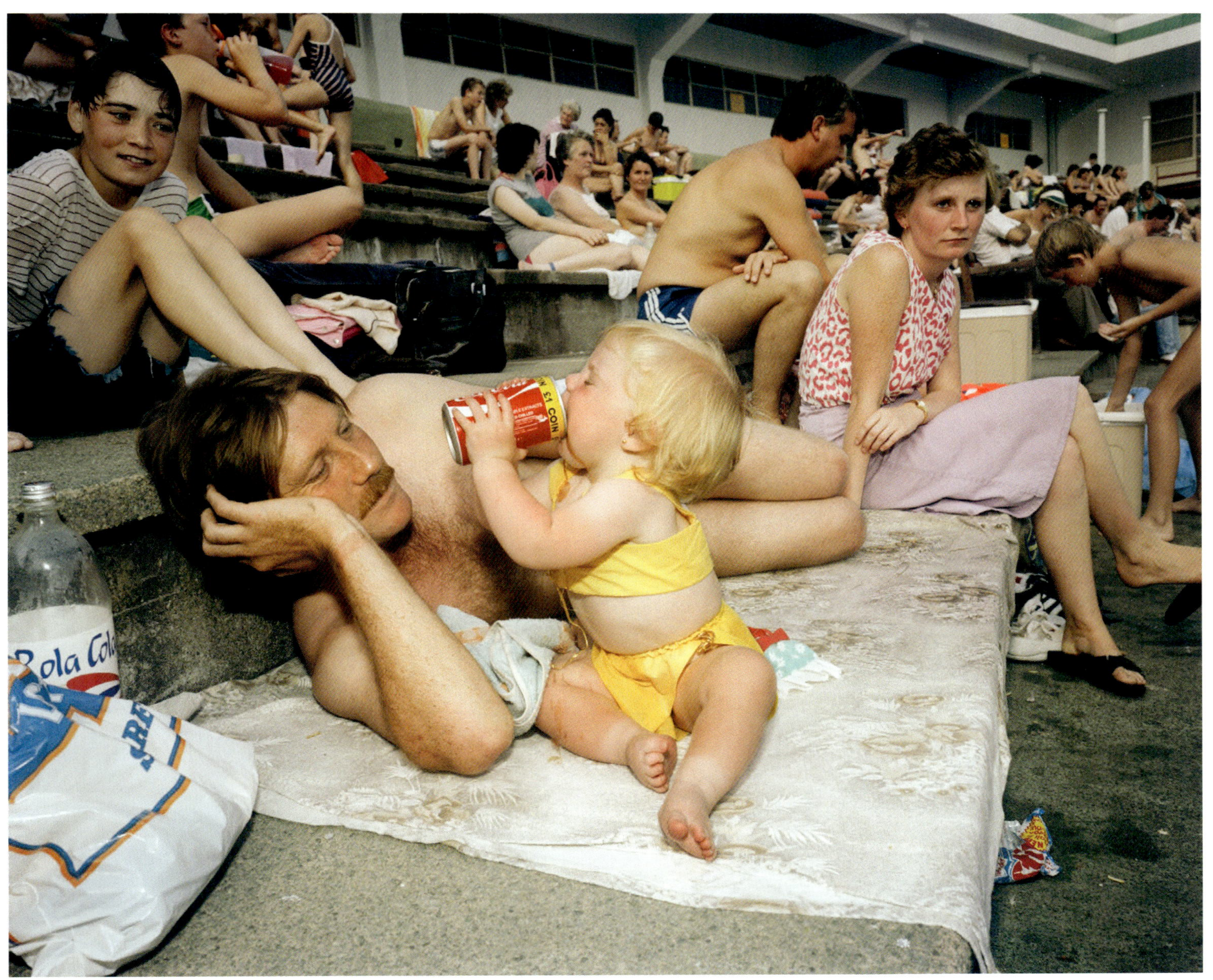

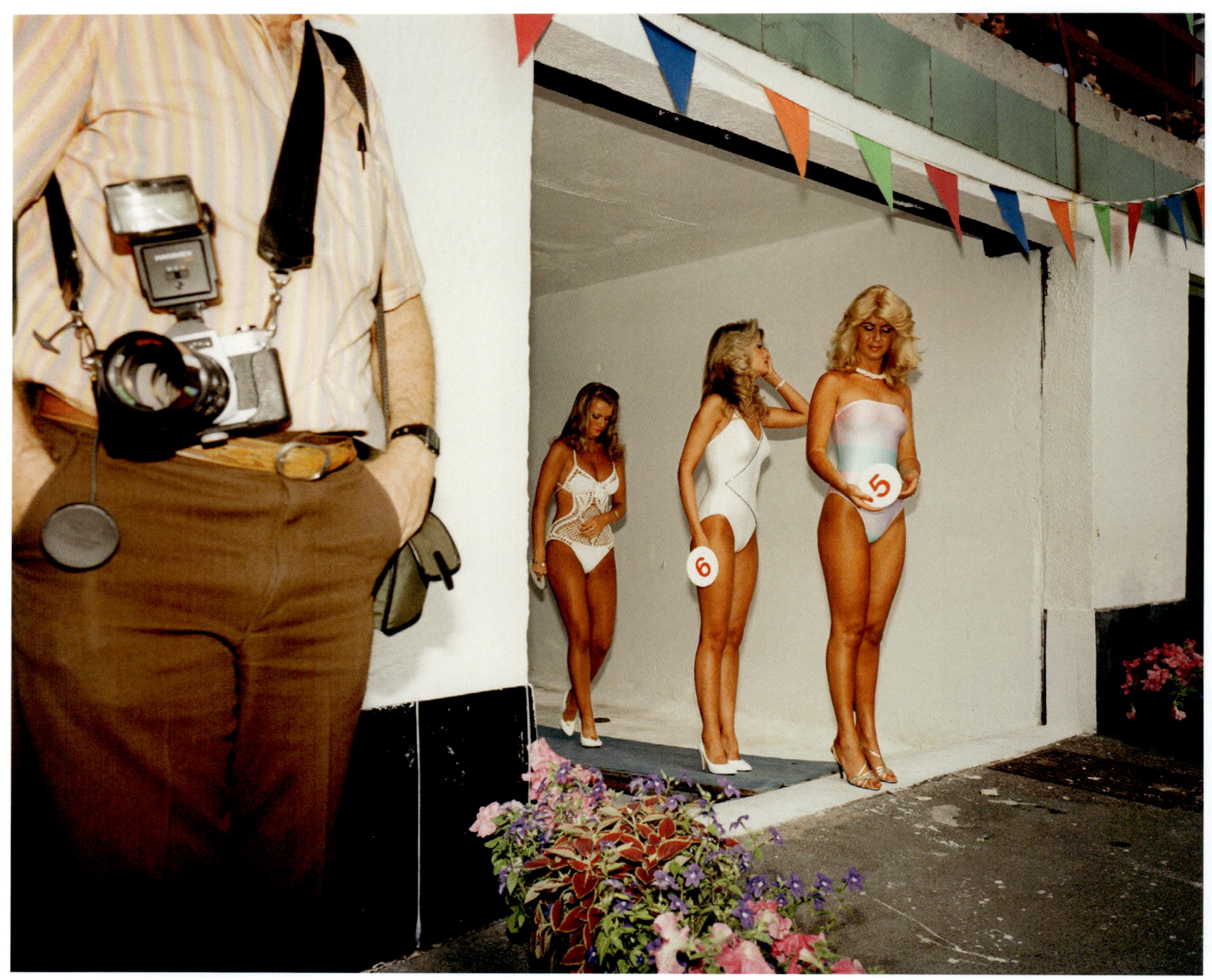

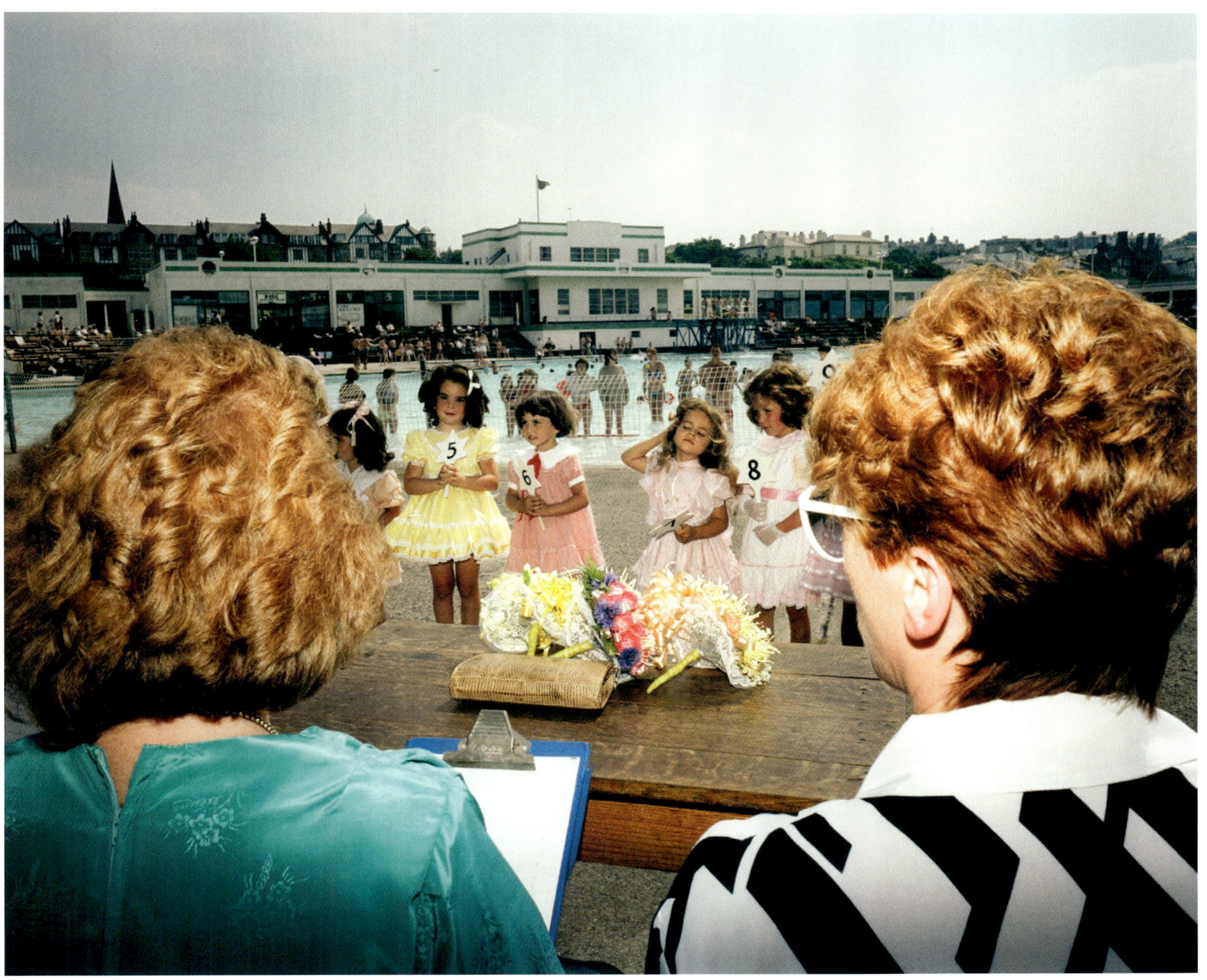

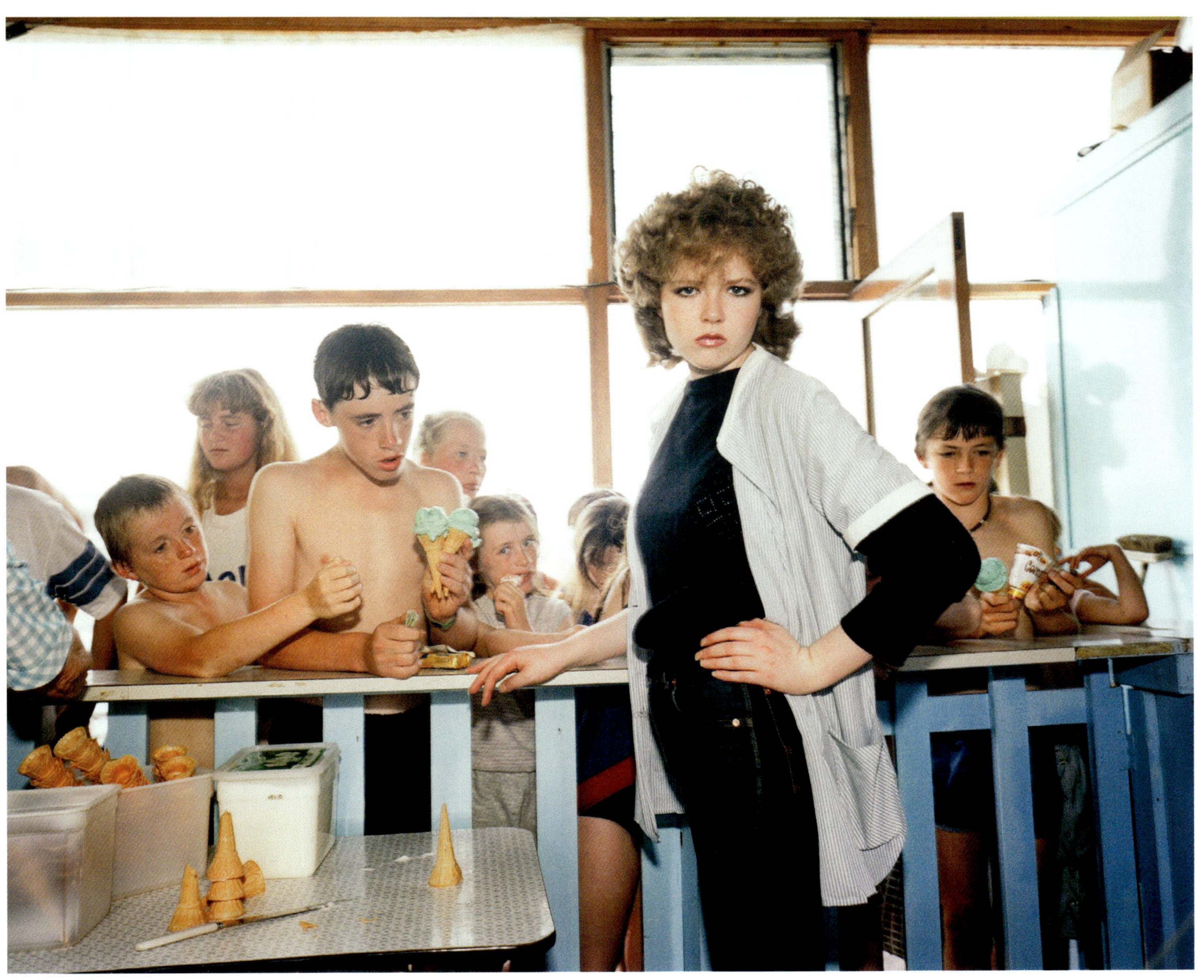

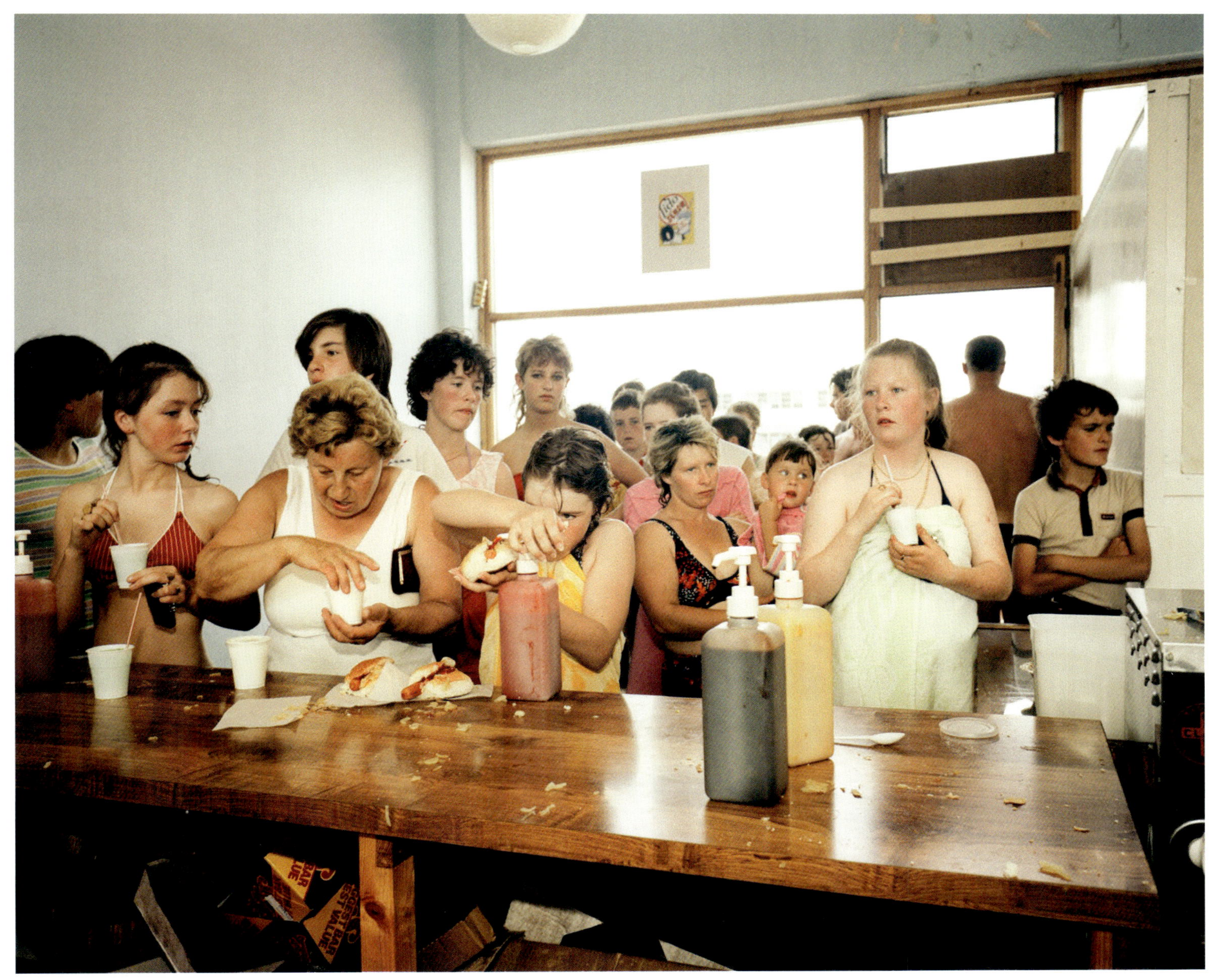

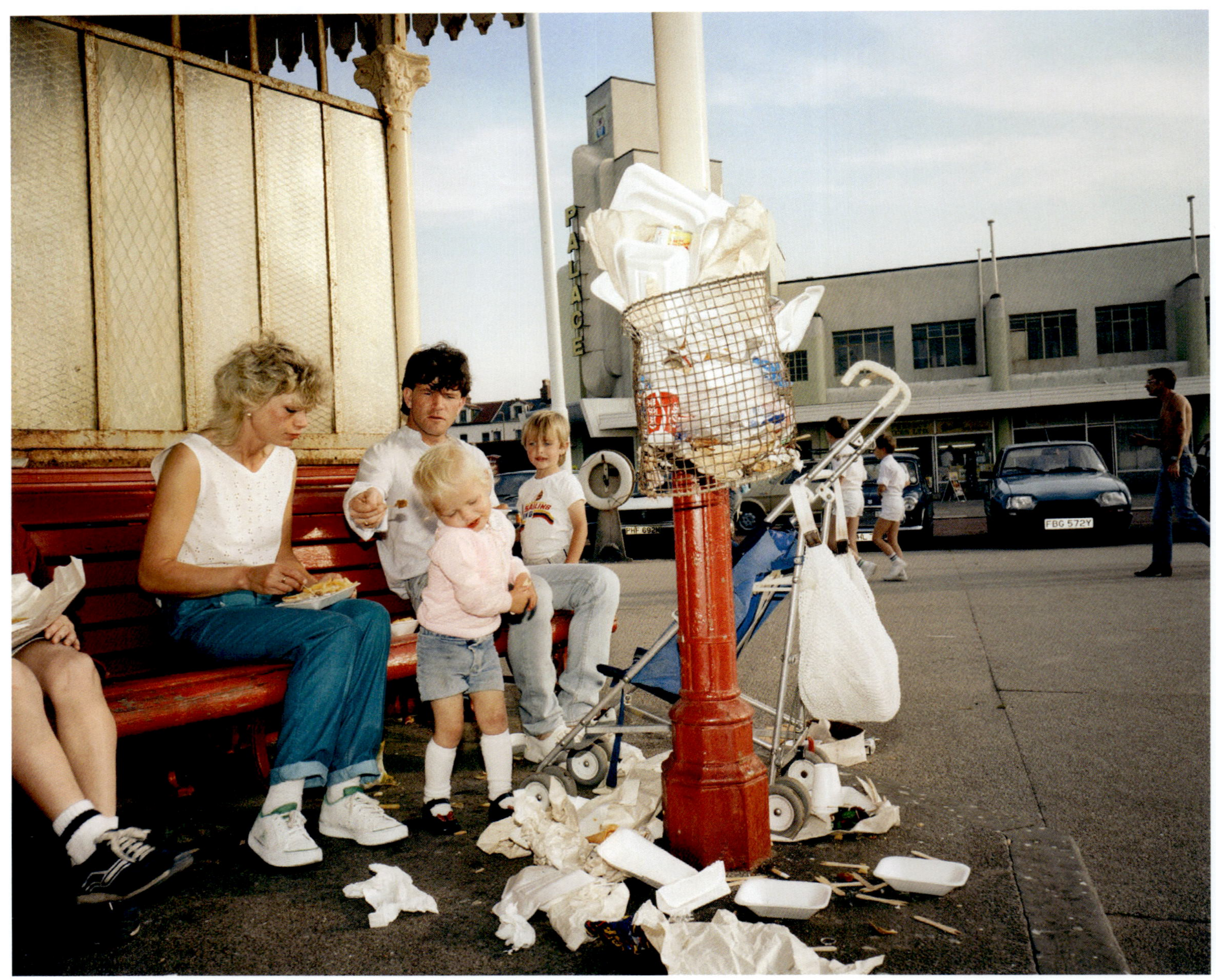

PALACE
PHF 692H
FBG 572Y

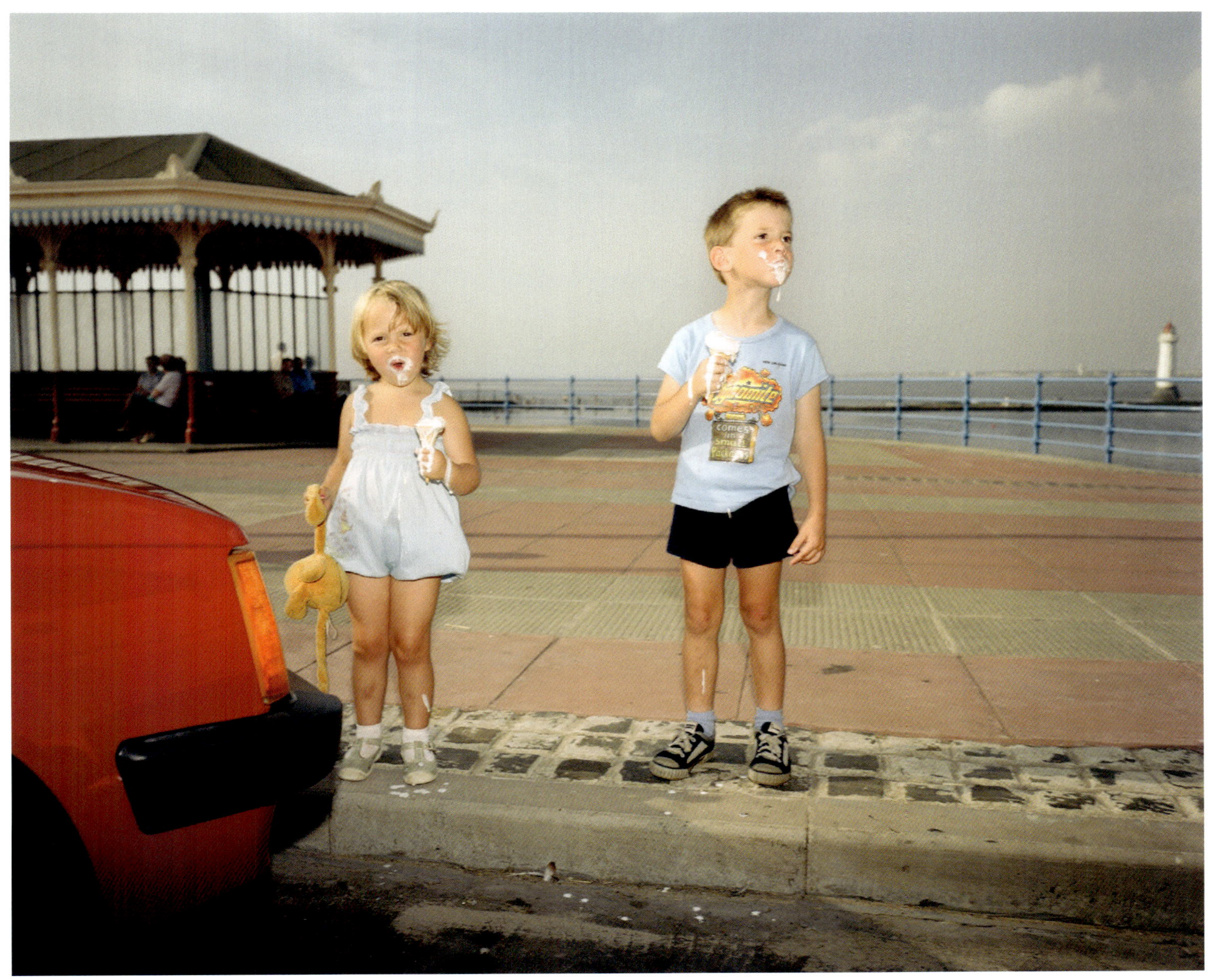

Cornetto
comes in small packs

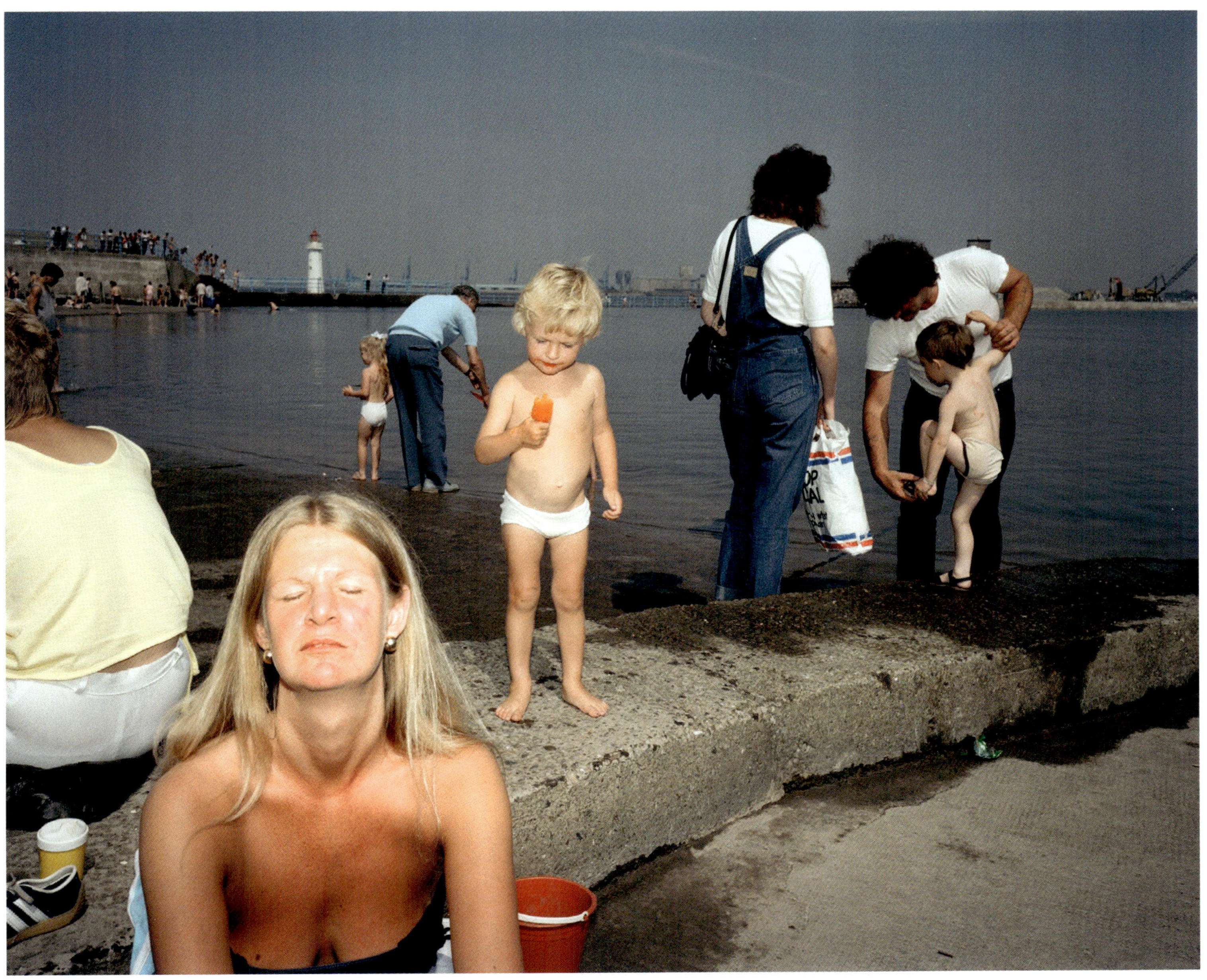

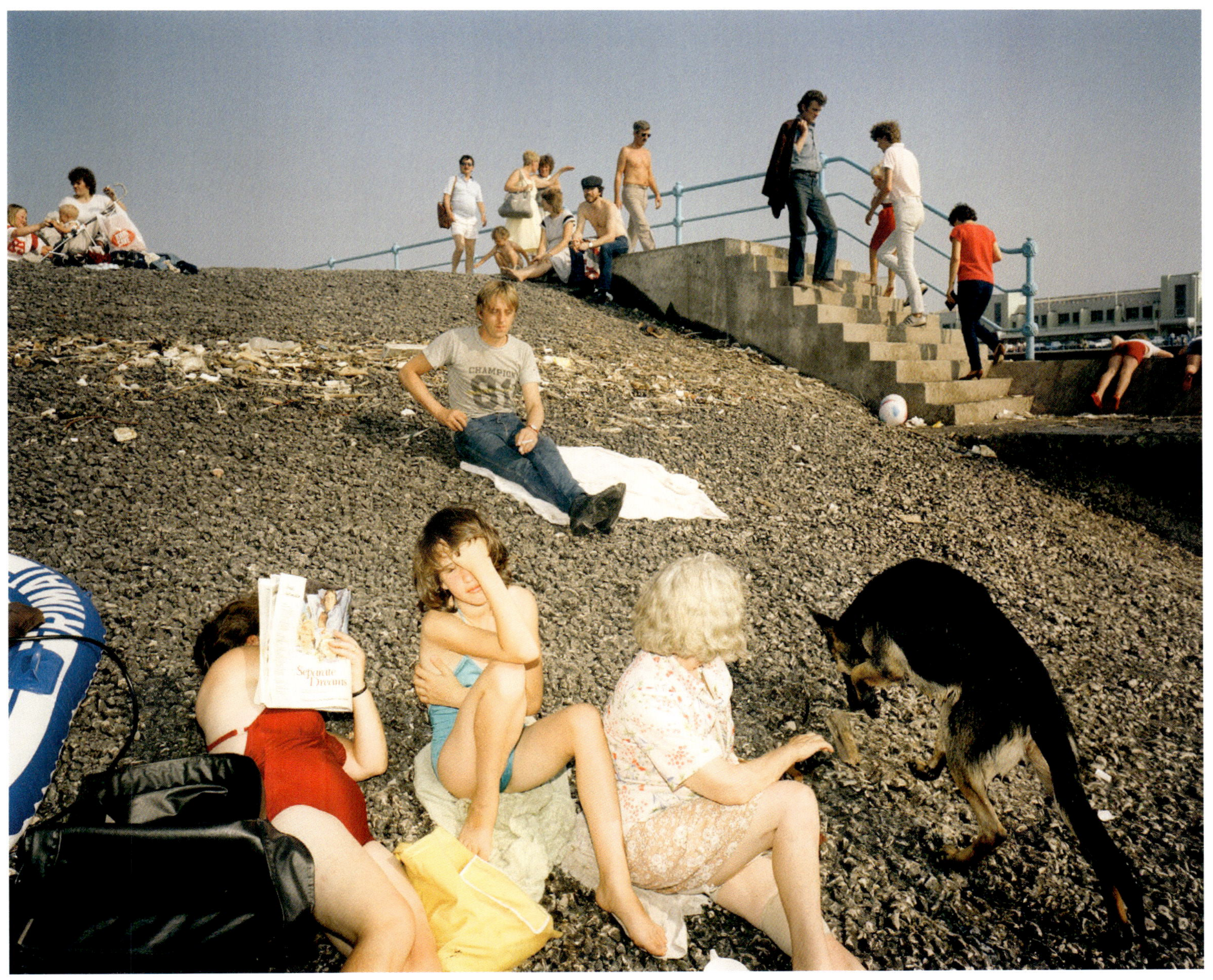

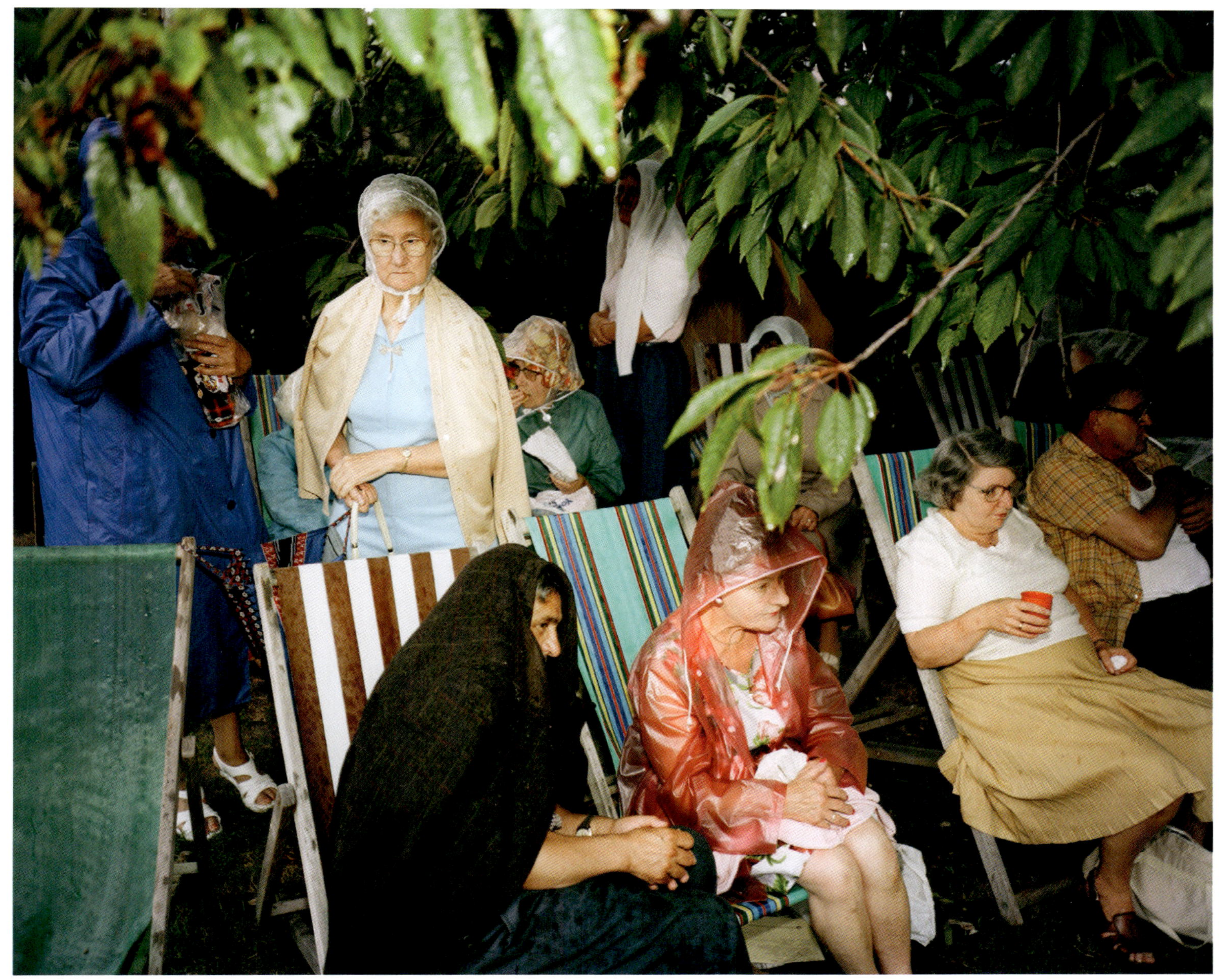

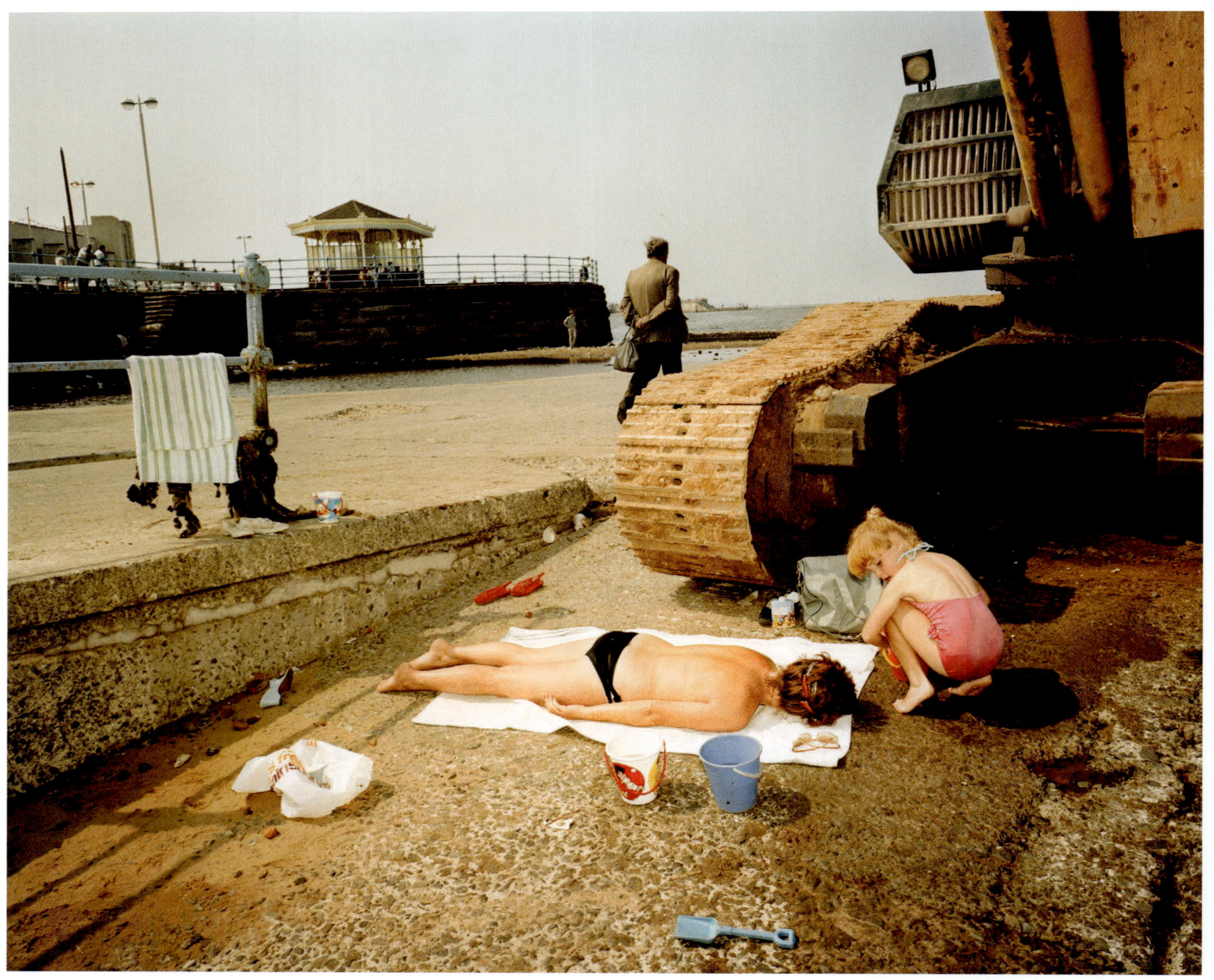

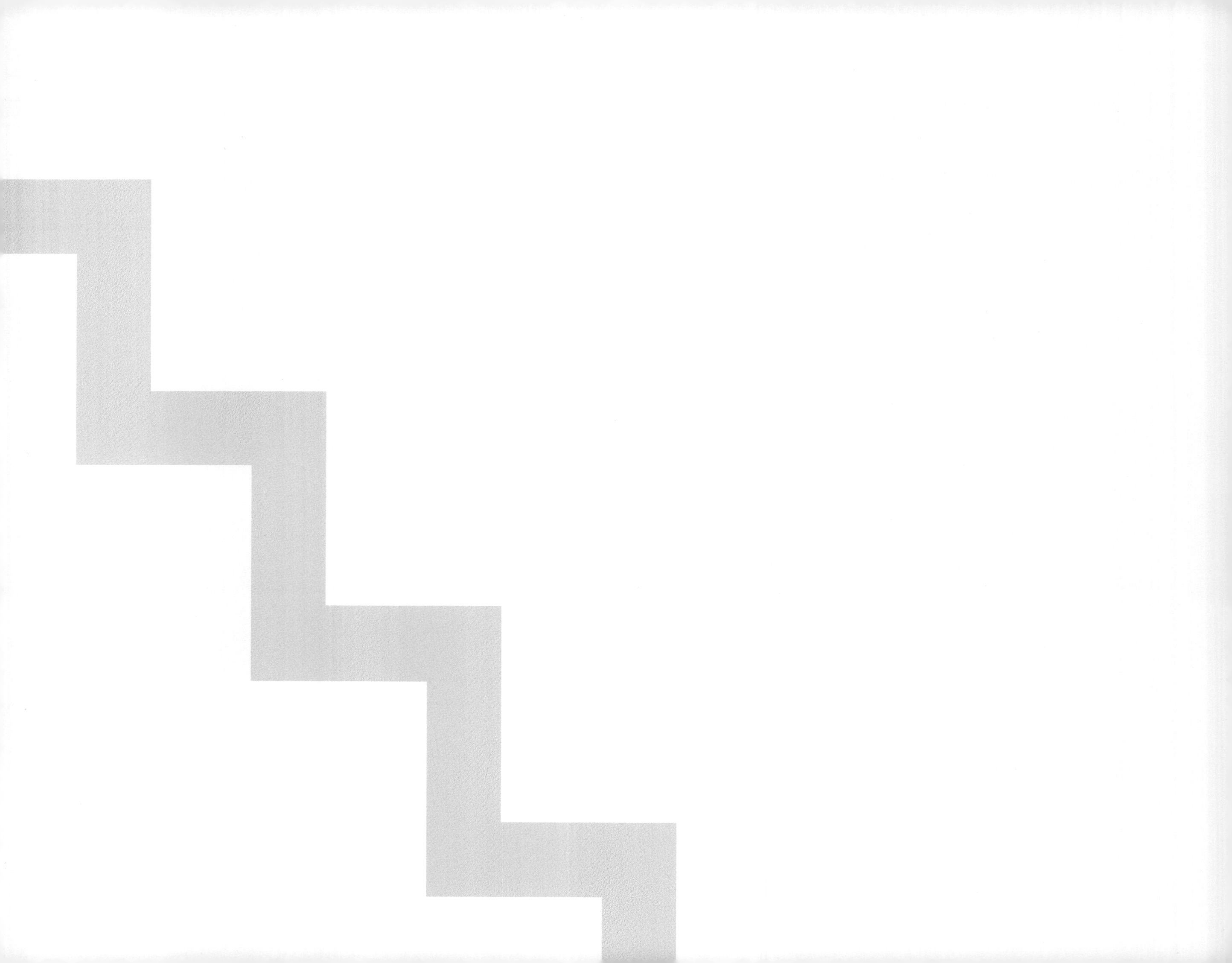

More Was More: Working with Martin Parr on *The Last Resort*
Peter Brawne

Martin Parr self-published the first edition of *The Last Resort: Photographs of New Brighton* under the imprint Promenade Press (taken from his then address at Egremont Promenade) in 1986. But of course its origins go back earlier. Midway through the interminable 11-and-a-half years of prime minister Margaret Thatcher's Conservative party rule, Martin had been in touch about the book I was to subsequently design. But this wasn't the first (or last) photo-book I was to work on with Martin. Two years previously Martin had asked me to design his second book, *A Fair Day: Photographs from the West of Ireland* (Promenade Press, 1984). The book acts as a showcase for a series of elegiac black and white photos, the last before his move into the colour pictures for which he is better known. To Martin I was untested, so by his own admission, when I worked on this book he kept me on a tight rein. Its appearance was competent but not original. It broke few rules and followed many of the orthodoxies of previously published books of monochrome photography.

Having proved myself with *A Fair Day*, on *The Last Resort* Martin took a leap of faith: I recall him saying 'go mad'. So on this project the reins were off and I took him at his word. Such a degree of freedom between client and designer was rare and much appreciated. I saw the photos and knew that something other than the formulaic approach common to many photo-books was required. But there were some limits to what was possible. All the photographs were

landscape format, so this practically demanded a landscape format book. Martin wanted each of the 40 photos the same size in a sequence in which each would occupy a double-page spread by itself. This made it obvious that photos should appear on right-hand pages, the first thing you saw – the main event – as you turned over from the previous page. This 'rule' was broken in just three places where a photo appears on both a right- and a left-hand page as they had clear visual connections with each other. There were also some old postcards of New Brighton Martin wanted to reproduce: one appears on the half-title page, another at the foot of the first page of Ian Walker's six-page essay at the start of the book, and the final on the last page.

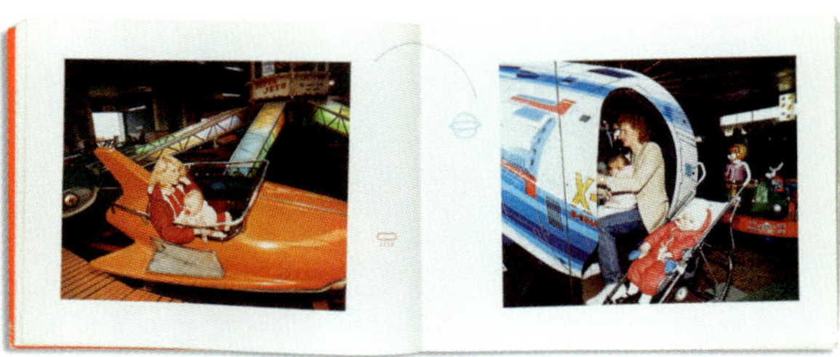

fig. 1. Double page spread from *The Last Resort* photobook, published 1986
© Martin Parr Collection / Magnum Photos

Within these parameters I looked for elements within each photo that suggested some sort of graphic response. I used the white space around the photos to do this. For instance, on page six (a

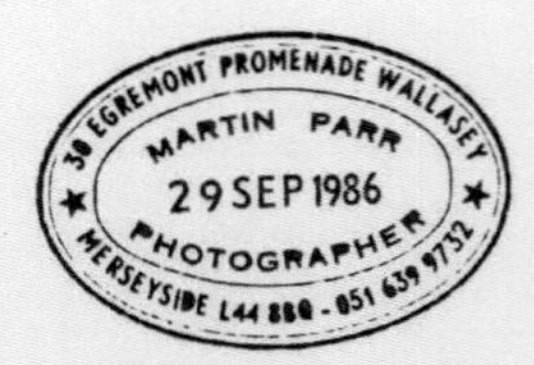

Dear Peter,

Thanks for letter + invoice — I'd forgotten about it (sadly!)

Regretfully you are too far advanced for the public and most people have not liked the 'shapes', The covers and all other aspects have been widely admired. I still like it, but prefer some pages to others.

Can you return to me the set of 40 10"×8" machine prints in due course.

Best wishes

Martin.

fig. 4. Handwritten letter from Martin Parr to Peter Brawne, 1986.
Courtesy of Peter Brawne.

left-hand page) (fig. 1) is a photo of a woman holding a baby on a fairground 'Super Jets' ride in a space-age type vehicle that looks (but isn't) suspended in mid-air. To the right of this photo I added a curved horizontal shape with four squiggles underneath like a simple diagram of a hover-car. On the adjacent page a photo shows a man on another fairground ride holding a girl within something that looks like a space rocket. So in the area to the left of the photo I placed a shape like a gyroscope or the outline of an orbit around a planet. Each page or spread required a different response. Some of these can be seen more or less literally. For instance, page 23 shows a mass of orangey-yellow squares like the chips on the counter of the fish and chip shop in the photo; others are less so, being more abstract or tangential.

Martin was always straightforward to work with. He wasn't brusque, but he was no-nonsense, businesslike and decisive. At the time of *The Last Resort* he was living and working in Wallasey, a suburb of Liverpool, close to New Brighton where he took the pictures for the book; I was living in Hackney and working at a shared studio with a couple of other photographers, Edward Barber (1949-2017) and Paul Trevor, that we'd set up in Paul's flat off Brick Lane in Tower Hamlets, east London. Both Ed and Paul had been involved with Camerawork – a magazine, darkroom and exhibition space – and its precursor, the Half Moon Photography Workshop, alongside other photographers including Jenny Matthews, Jo Spence (1934–1992) and Mike Goldwater. Paul already knew Martin and though I can't remember where or when, I'm sure it would have been him that originally introduced (or suggested) me to Martin. It was at this East London studio that *The Last Resort* was designed.

Though Martin and I met in person on a few occasions in Wallasey

or London, the bulk of our interactions involved corresponding by post. It must have been on one of our rare meetings that Martin showed me another landscape format photo-book, John Gossage's *The Pond* (Aperture, 1985) on which the super-graphics style title wraps around from back to front cover (fig 2). This precedent seemed to grant permission for a cover without a photo and treating the book's title extremely boldly (fig 3).

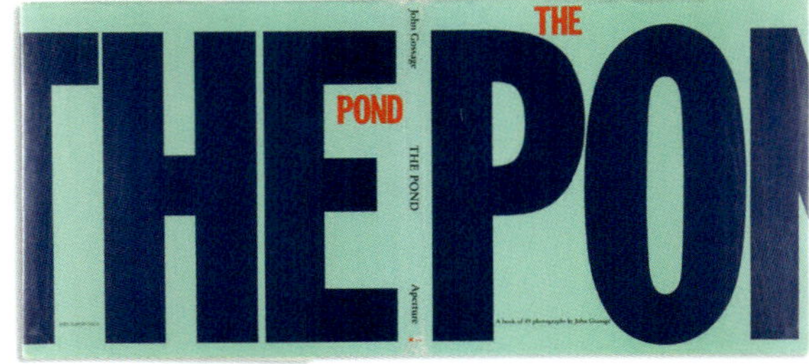

fig. 2. Wraparound book cover for *The Pond* by John Gossage, published by Aperture, 1985. Design by Gabriele Goetz.

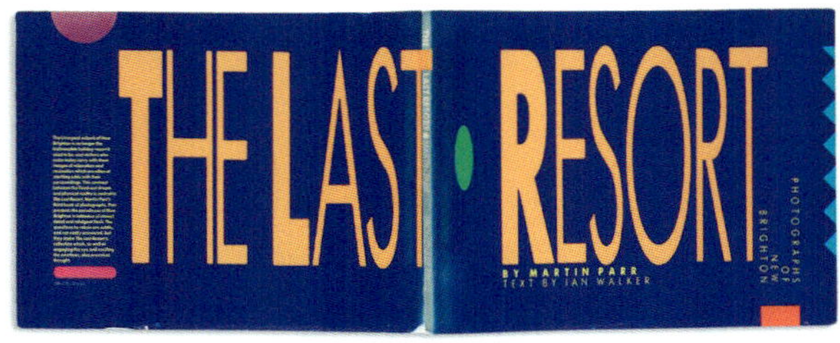

fig. 3. Wraparound book cover for *The Last Resort* by Martin Parr, published by Martin Parr under Promenade Press, 1986. Design by Peter Brawne.

When letters from Martin arrived – hand-written, often on checked notepad-paper with the inked impression from a rubber-stamp at the top that carried his name and address – they were always succinct and to the point (fig 4). The process of putting the book together

was a to-and-fro, inevitably slower than it would be today (typically
emails with attachments) reliant as it was then on the Royal Mail.
Making artwork at that time was also very different. Today I'd sit at
a computer; then I stood in front of a parallel motion drawing board
with copies of the images and galleys of typesetting that I'd cut and
paste down onto a baseboard. The colour of the shapes on the inside
pages, or the dispersal of colour on the cover required tracing-paper
overlays to highlight and specify to the printer which colour went
where on the elements visible beneath.

In any case, I now wince at much of what I did then. The need I felt
at that time to graphically intervene seems misjudged. The 'shapes'
appear superfluous, excessive, self-indulgent; the typography,
overblown and mannered. On the other hand, the colour plates – the
great bulk of the book – were very well reproduced by the original
printer, Jackson Wilson in Leeds, accurately capturing in print what
Martin had caught on film. Reconsidering the book now, I think I was
too susceptible to some of the trends that were current within English
design at that time: the follies of post-modernism with its penchant
for kitsch, whimsical decoration and a certain sort of colour palette
(though many of these colours do appear in the photos); doing things
that were newly possible – for instance artificially condensing type
(shown in extremis on the book's cover) – rather than adding or
subtracting something that would contribute beneficially to the whole.

That said, the book is very much a product of its time and was
perhaps just what Martin needed. In his shift from black and white
to colour he and the images that are captured in this book made a
loud, dramatic and decisive splash. It also proved to be the critical
launchpad for the trailblazing photography that Martin would
subsequently go on to make.

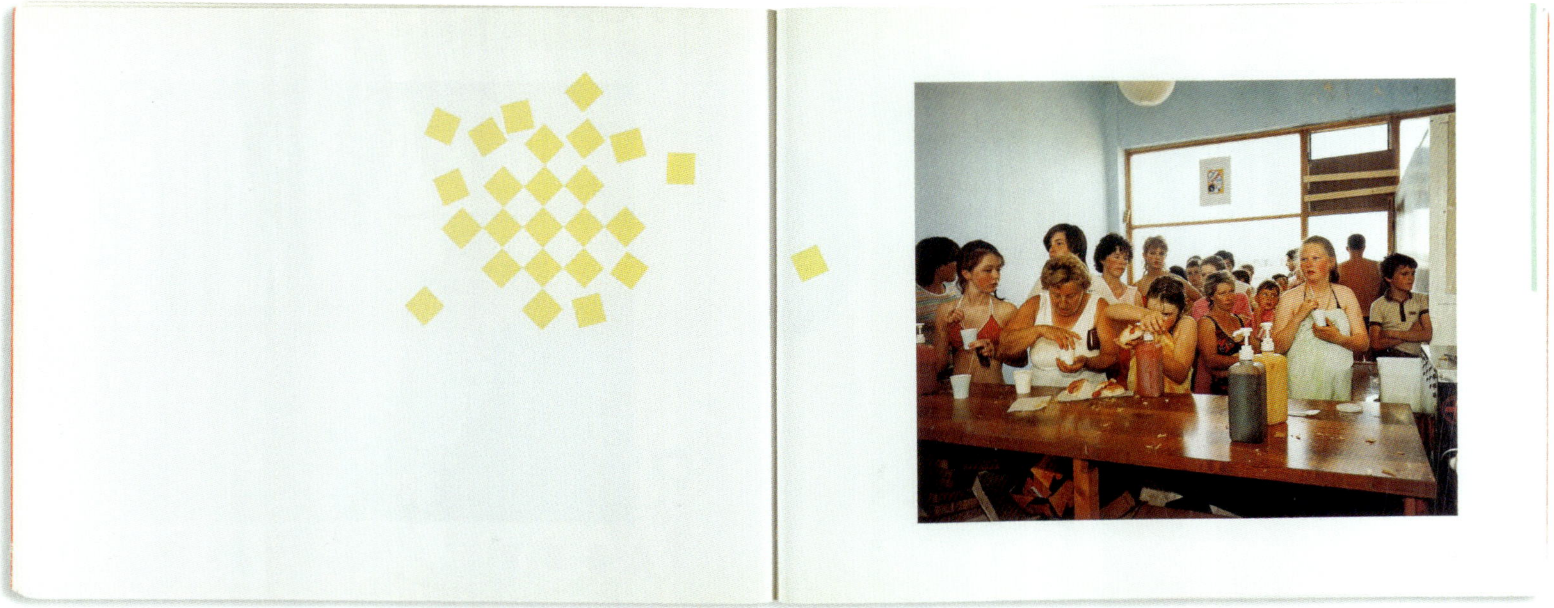

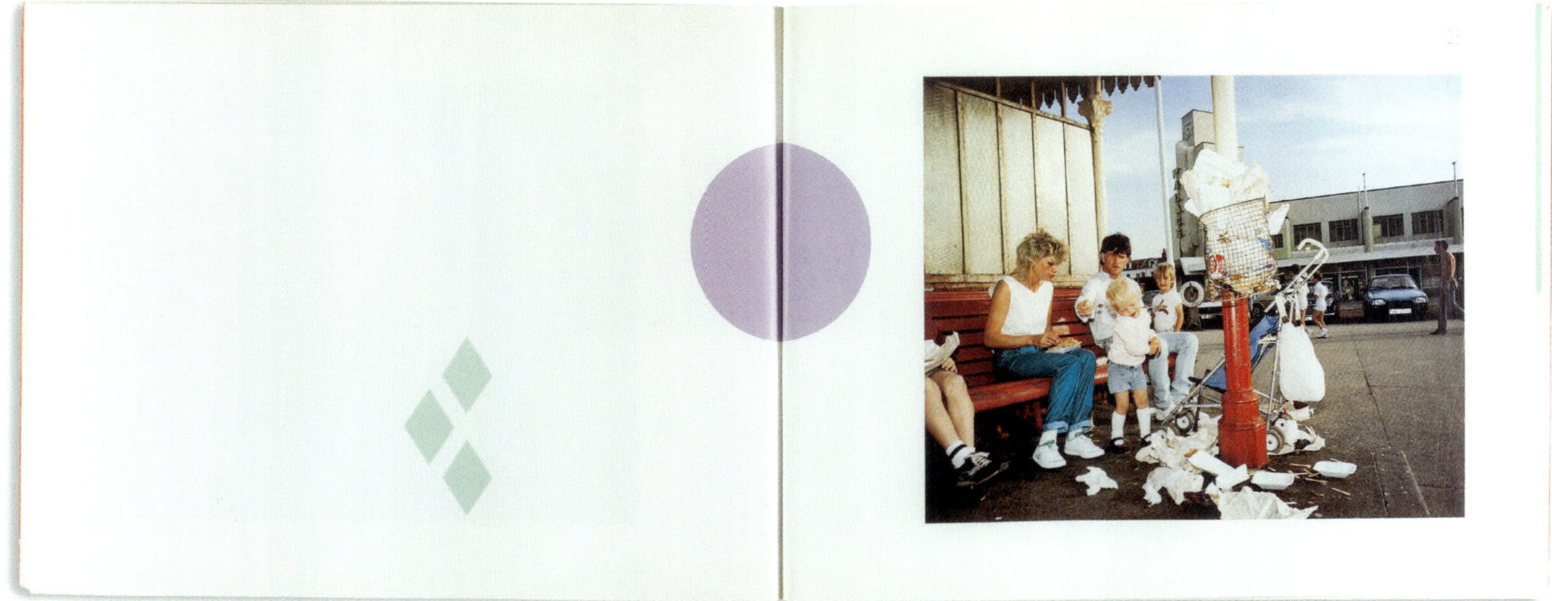

Double page spreads from *The Lcst Resort* photobook, published by Promenade Press, 1986 © Martin Parr Collection / Magnum Photos

Martin Parr
Contact Sheets

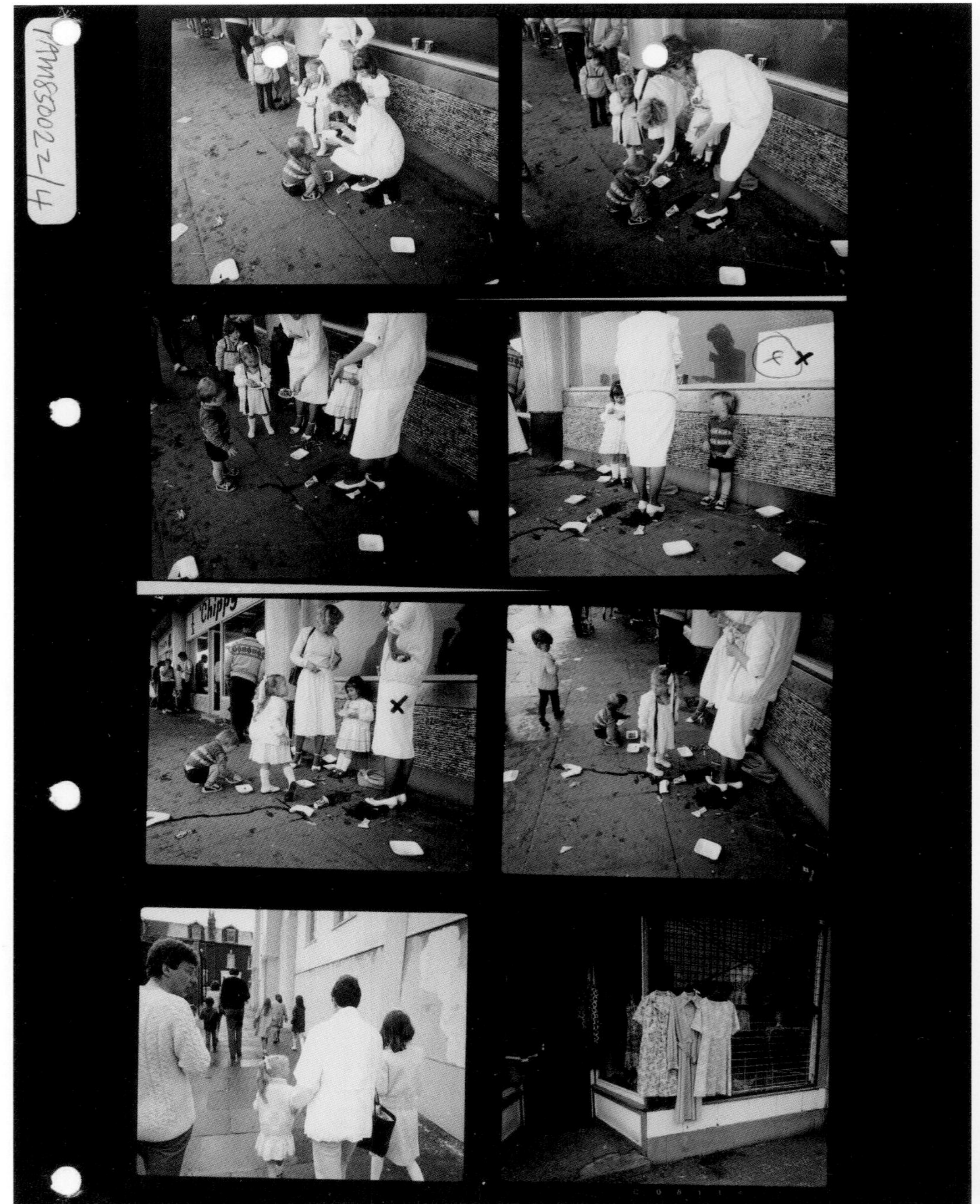

Martin Parr contact sheet from *The Last Resort*, 1983-85
© Martin Parr Collection / Magnum Photos

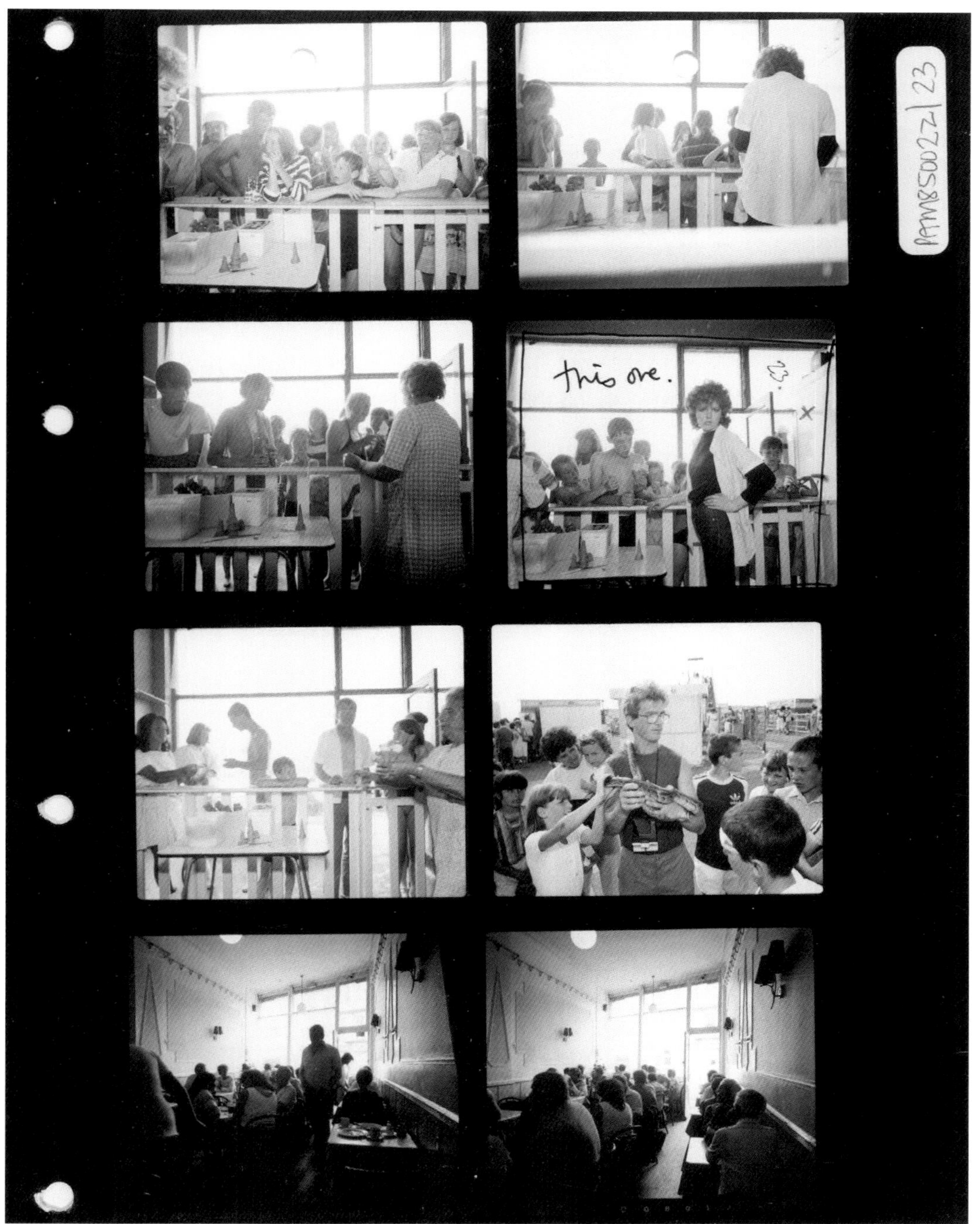

Martin Parr contact sheet from *The Last Resort*, 1983-85
© Martin Parr Collection / Magnum Photos

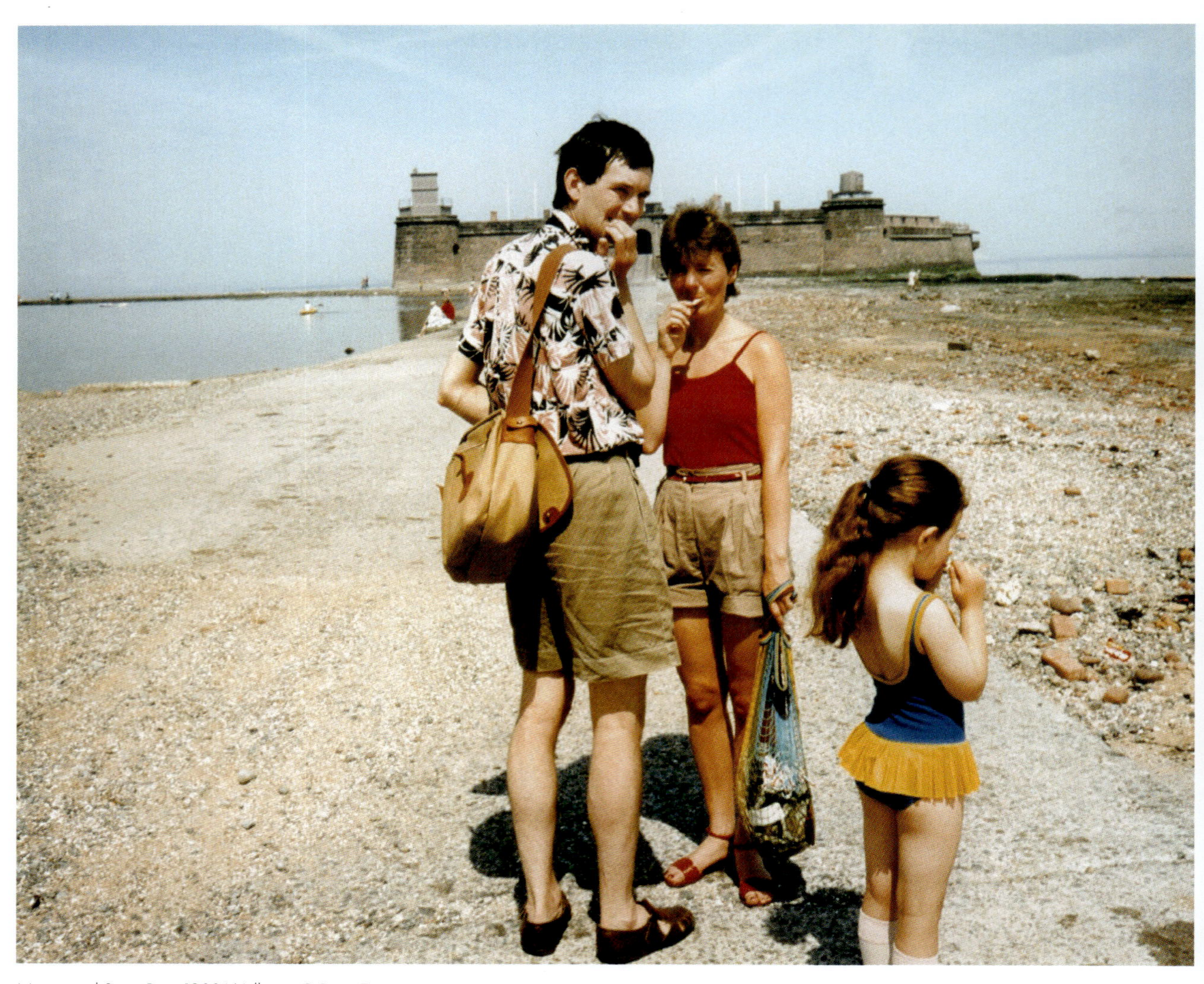

Martin and Susie Parr, 1983 Wallasey © Peter Fraser

Afterword
Susie Parr

When we moved from Ireland to Liverpool in 1982, we bought a house on Egremont Promenade in Wallasey. It was a Victorian pile with fantastic views of the Mersey. I would roller skate down the prom to catch the ferry and take the no 84 bus to work. Martin would cycle the other way to New Brighton. Having recently left the gorgeous beaches and clean seas of the West of Ireland, I personally found New Brighton a bit much, what with all the pollution and litter. It was incredibly run down, truly a sign of the times in Thatcher's Britain.

Having been very fond of Martin's more elegiac black and white work in Hebden Bridge and Ireland, the brash colour of his images was a shock. But I could see that it was an extraordinary body of work. When the show opened at the Open Eye Gallery in Liverpool in the winter of 1985, guests dressed appropriately, with rain hats, swimming costumes, lilos and pac-a-macs. No one batted an eyelid at the images: that was what New Brighton was like. It is a well documented fact that the response to the show at The Serpentine was rather different.

As regards the images themselves, in my view they are full of affection and humanity. Martin truly loved New Brighton. Indeed he requested that his ashes be scattered on the beach there. This we will do around the time of his birthday in May, the best month of the year.

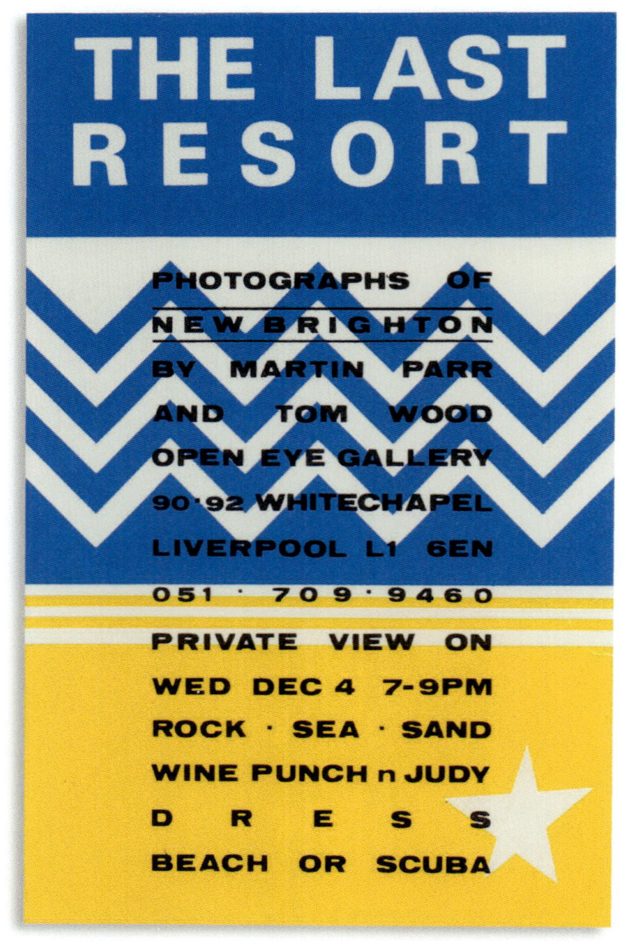

The Last Resort opening invitation for the Open Eye Gallery exhibition, Liverpool, 1985 © Martin Parr Collection / Magnum Photos

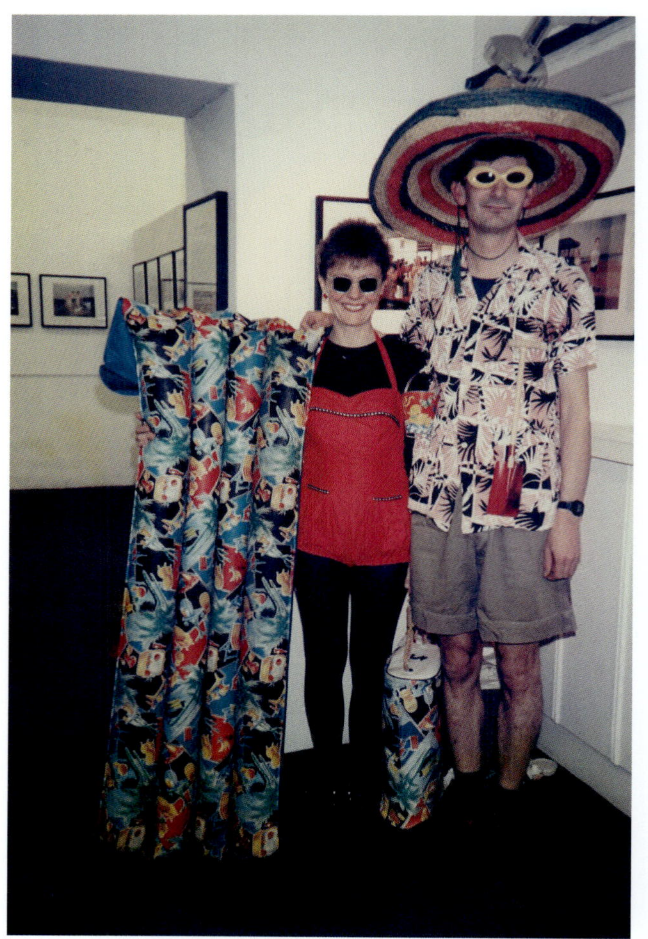

Martin and Susie Parr at the opening of *The Last Resort*, Open Eye Gallery, Liverpool, 1985 © Martin Parr Collection / Magnum Photos

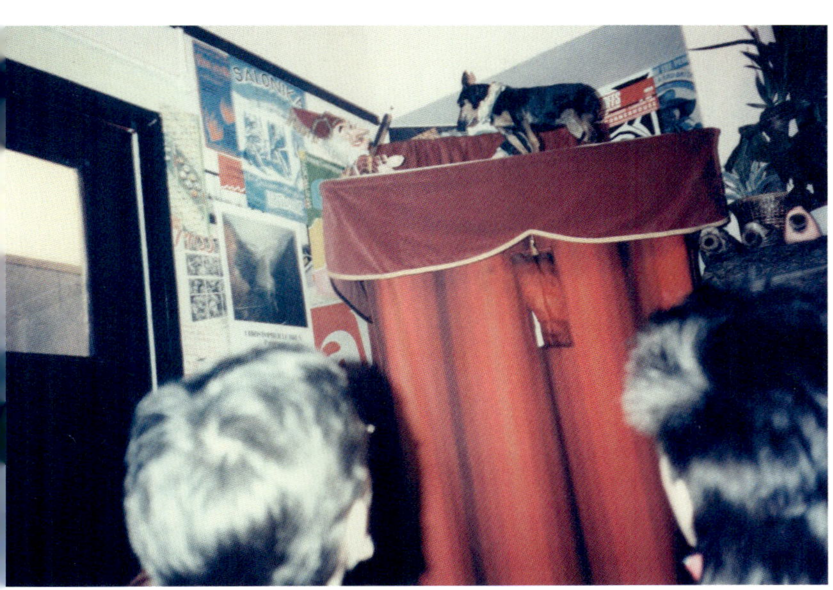

Punch and Judy show at the opening of *The Last Resort*, Open Eye Gallery, Liverpool, 1985
© Martin Parr Collection / Magnum Photos

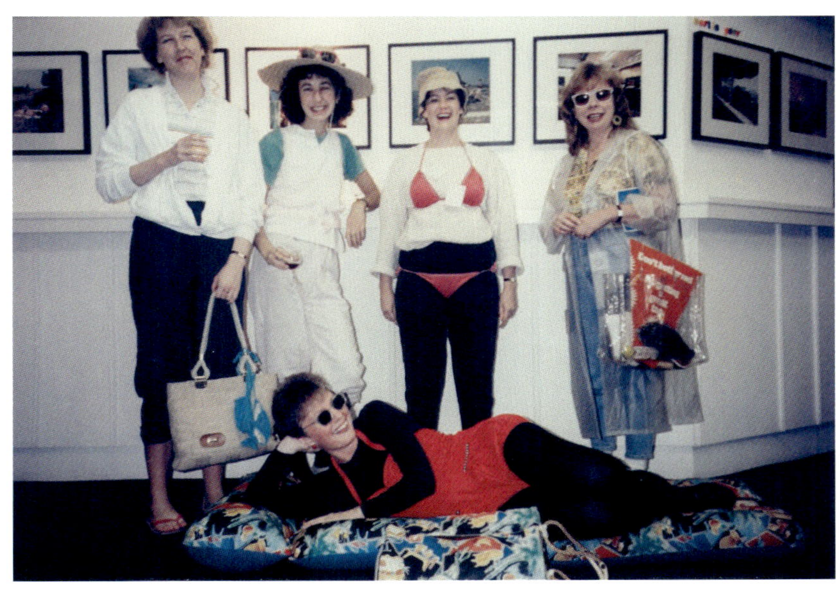

Susie Parr and friends at the opening of *The Last Resort*, Open Eye Gallery, Liverpool, 1985
© Martin Parr Collection / Magnum Photos

THE LAST RESORT
40 YEARS ON

Co-published by Martin Parr Foundation and Dewi Lewis Publishing, 2026. This exhibition and publication celebrate the remarkable career of Martin Parr (1952-2025).

MPF

Produced to coincide with *The Last Resort, 40 Years On*, exhibited at the Martin Parr Foundation in Bristol, 2026. Thank you to the MPF team for the work in bringing together this exhibition and publication.

Plates - New Brighton, England, 1983-85. From *The Last Resort* © Martin Parr / Magnum Photos

Texts by Isaac Blease, Peter Brawne and Susie Parr

All texts © the authors

Design by Nathan Vidler

First edition, printed by Taylor Brothers, Bristol

ISBN / 978-1-916915-21-3

Typeface as originally used by Peter Brawne, and geometric colour shapes originally designed by Peter Brawne, for the first publication of *The Last Resort*, 1986.

This exhibition and accompanying publication also mark the 40th anniversary of The Last Resort, first published and exhibited as a solo show in 1986. The original photobook was self-published by Martin Parr under Promenade Press and designed by Peter Brawne. Dewi Lewis went on to publish subsequent editions of the photobook in 1998 and 2009. The work was initially shown at Open Eye Gallery, Liverpool, in a joint exhibition with Tom Wood in the winter of 1985, ahead of Martin's landmark solo exhibition of The Last Resort at Serpentine Gallery, London, in 1986.